EAT
MORE
VEGAN!

80 AMAZING PLANT-BASED DISHES

EAT MORE VEGAN!

LUKE HINES

plum.   Pan Macmillan Australia

This book is dedicated to anyone who wants to better their health with real food in the most delicious way – and have fun doing it.

CONTENTS

INTRODUCTION

If there's one thing on this earth that we all have in common, it's the fact that each and every one of us should be putting more plants on our plate. So, for this exciting milestone – my tenth cookbook – it seems fitting that I'm celebrating an abundance of plant-based foods. Because, let's be honest, we could all eat more vegan!

We are so fortunate to be living in an age where information about how to live our healthiest and happiest lives is readily available to us. But the best news is that we can use this information not only for our own benefit, but also for the benefit of the world that we share with everyone and everything around us. Supported by the latest research and science, we can see first-hand the impact that our meat-dominant eating habits are having on both the health of our bodies and that of the environment, so it makes sense that a new way of thinking about plant-based eating is emerging.

This book demonstrates how eating more plants is great for your health, and also shows you how easy it can be to add new flavours and an abundance of colour, texture and life to your plate with just a few simple techniques.

Other important issues to consider when it comes to celebrating a plant-based life include food security, the treatment of animals, industrialised farming practices and the long-term sustainability of current food production. As valid as each of these issues is, as a functional nutritionist, my key focus is your health. One of the biggest driving forces behind this book is to get everyone who picks it up to eat more plants and, in turn, improve your health with each mouthful.

So, what does my take on plant-based eating look like? First off, it's mostly packet free! I've kept the ingredients here pure, simple and real, which means seasonal fruits and vegetables, nuts and seeds, healthy cooking fats and oils, and an abundance of flavoursome, health-boosting herbs and spices. Considering optimal gut health starts with a broad spectrum of fruits and vegetables of all colours, shapes and sizes, these choices alone will have you on your way to thriving inside and out.

To maintain consistency with my overall approach to eating, I have also kept the recipes and ingredients aligned to my nutrient-dense, sustainable food philosophy while remaining as simple as possible without any time-consuming preparation. Therefore, I can proudly say this book is low carb, keto friendly, paleo and gluten-, dairy- and refined-sugar free. You won't find any faux versions of meats or meat replacements, which can often be high in soy and inflammatory seed oils. This book really does epitomise the real food movement in the most authentic way.

I haven't included beans, legumes, grains and pseudo grains in the book, as without adequate and time-consuming preparation such as sprouting and fermenting, they can cause digestive issues. By avoiding these foods, I am steering you away from potentially high levels of phytic acid and lectins. Phytic acid binds to nutrients in our food, preventing us from absorbing them. And lectins can damage the intestinal wall, contributing to leaky gut, with all its associated digestive problems. While I believe health is always individual, and there is no one-size-fits-all approach, what I do believe in is celebrating nutrient density and reducing inflammation. That is why I only use ingredients in this book that are proven to increase your wellness and stave off any digestive issues or inflammatory responses.

While each recipe in this book is designed to deliver epic levels of nutrients and flavour, I also want you to find confidence in the kitchen, and that means making sure these meals are as doable as they are delicious. Everyone is different when it comes to tastes and preferences, so please navigate this book in a way that works for you. I recommend cooking in bulk to have more on hand later, only adding dressings to salads once you're about to eat them to retain freshness, and keeping things simple in the kitchen by picking a few key ingredients and making them shine. On a technical note, all oven temperatures stated are fan-forced, so if you have a conventional oven you'll need to increase the temperature by about 20°C, but please note that cooking times may vary depending on your individual oven.

I strongly believe that every meal we consume is a chance to not only triumphantly say 'yum' after each mouthful, but is also an opportunity to steer us closer to living our best lives. With good food comes a good body, both inside and out, and by simply eating more vegan, you will find it easier than ever before to achieve this.

My promise to you is that, in my quest to make you healthier, I will never sacrifice flavour. And my final words are these: have fun! Food is one of the simplest pleasures we have in life, so ditch the calorie counting, celebrate abundance, listen to your body and smile.

Luke xx

WHO IS THIS BOOK FOR?

Eat More Vegan **isn't just for vegans. It's for everyone! All of us need to be eating more plants and improving our health with nutrient-dense real food. So, whether you are vegan, vegetarian, paleo, low carb or keto, every recipe here is suitable for you. That said, let's take a closer look at how to make this book work best for you, depending on where you sit on the eating spectrum.**

VEGANS AND VEGETARIANS

If you are vegan or vegetarian, I know you are just going to love this book! Plant-based cooking should be delicious and nutritious, and the recipes within these pages have been designed to give you maximum flavour as well as an abundance of nutrients.

Speaking as a nutritional therapist, for anyone following a 100 per cent plant-based diet I need to highlight the importance of combining your foods each day for optimal nutrient diversity to ensure you don't miss out on any of the key components to wellness. So, for example, making sure that each day you are well hydrated and that your food intake is diverse enough that you get all the protein, healthy fats, well-sourced carbs and fibre you need to function at your very best. I also recommend you take good-quality vitamin B12, iron and zinc supplements as these can be harder to source and absorb in plant-based diets. For optimal health, it is key to make sure you're getting all of the essential macro and micronutrients on board, so please feel free to add to any of my recipes in whatever way you know benefits you and your body to help you thrive on an individual level.

REDUCETARIANS

Some of you who currently consume animal meats and fats might want ways to reduce your daily intake of these and increase your daily dose of 'greens', so to speak. Becoming a 'reducetarian' is a fantastic stepping stone for people who are considering a long-term plant-based lifestyle or for those who want to reduce their 'meat' footprint on the world (or both).

It is important to note that if you choose to eat meat and dairy, there are a few things to consider. Some farming practices can be cruel to animals and harmful to the environment, so it's important to be mindful of where you source your meat and dairy. Encouragingly, there are a number of producers within the agriculture industry who are trying to change the standards of animal production to regulate for the most humane methods possible. Without their passion and commitment, change cannot happen, so please vote with your dollar and look for organic, free-range, grass-fed and pasture-raised livestock and dairy products.

HEALTH ENTHUSIASTS

I nickname the people in this category the 'Just Get Me Healthy Crew'. This category is for those who aren't necessarily vegan, and perhaps haven't given much thought to their animal consumption, but who are, nonetheless, passionate and committed to making long-term, delicious and sensible health changes.

If this is you, be aware that plants are full of the most incredible and powerful health-benefiting properties (which I will talk about in more detail shortly), and are key to unlocking better gut health, optimal digestion, improved energy and mood, and an elevated sense of overall wellbeing. So, if you've ever wanted to look, feel and be a better version of you, make this your new bible.

Lastly, whichever group you fit into, I ask that as you make your way through this book, you keep in mind that the better the quality of the fruits and vegetables you choose and the better the farming practices you support, the more you will notice improvements in your own personal health and wellbeing.

SO, WHY PLANTS?

Well, first off, plants are healthy and incredibly delicious! As a healthy cook, if I am to get you eating well long-term, my recipes need to pack a serious punch of flavour with every mouthful, so that's not a bad place to start. But there are some other pretty cool reasons why this book showcases plants, too.

First things first, plants are our only source of phytonutrients. These health-boosting compounds are responsible for plants' diverse and vibrant colours. Celebrating a wide variety of different fruits, vegetables and herbs means we get a lovely range of these essential nutrients into us, which helps to support the body's immunity, gut health, longevity and so much more.

Along with phytonutrients, there are a bunch of other nutrients that only plants can provide. Beta glucan, found in mushrooms, for example, is one of my favourites as it is not only a great source of fibre but is also an effective prebiotic, which can help us manage the way we absorb sugars, keeping our blood-sugar levels stable. Inulin, a prebiotic fibre found in asparagus, fresh herbs and bananas to name a few, helps promote good gut health and can keep us feeling fuller for longer. And, of course, resistant starch (see Health Tip, page 36) is a favourite of mine. Found in green papaya, green bananas and cooked and cooled root vegetables, it helps feed beneficial bacteria in the colon, promoting fantastic gut health as well as lowering the glycaemic load of higher carb vegetables.

Plants also carry many medicinal properties and have been used by various cultures for generations to aid in healing, immunity and overall good health. Simple, everyday ingredients such as turmeric, ginger and garlic have been chosen for their abilities to, respectively, reduce inflammation, relieve nausea and fight against bacterial and viral infections. Real food really is a wonderful source of medicine.

It is also an important time to do our bit for the environment and the world around us. To sustain our quality of life on this planet we need to give back to mother nature and be mindful of the impact of our choices. From how we vote with our shopping dollar by supporting ethical food manufacturing practices, to lessening our overall footprint in order to create a sustainable food culture for generations to come, now feels like the time for us to work together with the environment and eat more plant-based foods.

However you look at it, your body (and the planet) will thank you for making this particular investment in your long-term health.

THE PLANT-BASED PANTRY

Cooking with a diverse range of plant-based ingredients is incredibly exciting, as it offers up a whole world of nutrition and flavour. Having a well-stocked pantry, fridge and freezer is the best way to ensure you stay on track, as you'll always have the ingredients you need to whip up some delicious food.

ACID AND SALT

Good-quality acid and salt are essential to bringing out the flavour in all kinds of dishes. My top picks for healthy acids to keep in your pantry are apple cider vinegar, coconut cider vinegar, lemon juice and lime juice. I usually include these in sauces and dressings to help balance the overall flavour of each dish. Another simple way to incorporate healthy acids into your diet is to add a dash of apple cider vinegar or lemon juice to some filtered water to start your day. These acids help to stimulate the digestive system to better break down and absorb the nutrients in food. When it comes to salt, I use unrefined sea salt, as it contains beneficial minerals that have been stripped out of refined table salt.

CACAO

It is no secret that I am a lover of all things chocolate! But I also like to 'keep it real', so to speak! That means making my own from scratch using raw cacao butter, raw cacao powder and cacao nibs. Raw cacao butter is a great source of vitamins and minerals and a source of easy-to-use energy for our body. Cacao powder is rich in polyphenols, magnesium and antioxidants. Cacao nibs add great texture and crunch to recipes, while being rich in fibre, protein and healthy fats, too. Having cacao in all its forms on hand in your plant-based pantry will allow you to whip up delicious comforting drinks, quick and easy snacks, or even something more elaborate from the Treaty Eats chapter.

COCONUT

Coconut truly is a superfood in all its forms. From fresh young coconuts filled with electrolyte-rich water and delicious fatty flesh, to versatile coconut flour for binding and baking, and, of course, coconut milk and cream! Yum. Keep your house stocked with coconut oil for cooking; coconut aminos as a great soy sauce or tamari alternative; flour for baking; canned milk and cream for curries, drinks and sauces; and shredded and desiccated for crumbs, crusts and cakes. I also recommend keeping some MCT oil on hand. MCT stands for medium-chain triglycerides, and they're a very powerful form of healthy fat extracted from pure coconut oil. The strains of fat found in MCT oil (C8 and C10) bypass the liver when processed by our body and get delivered straight into our system, supplying us with a sustained energy source and contributing to hormonal balance and improved mood. In the recipes that follow I show you how to add it to a number of drinks, but it is also good drizzled over a finished meal, especially the salads in the Crispy and Crunchy chapter.

FLOURS

As you know, I follow a primal paleo approach to cooking and eating. That means my recipes exclude highly refined and high carbohydrate flours and baking aids. I highly recommend you stick to the gluten-free, nutrient-dense alternatives that I have suggested in these recipes to help you maintain stable blood sugar levels, reduce digestive dysfunction and keep you feeling great. My preferred choices are almond meal, hazelnut meal, coconut flour, arrowroot/tapioca flour, dried vegetable powders such as sweet potato powder, gluten-free and aluminium-free baking powder and bicarbonate of soda. You'll be amazed by how delicious and versatile these alternatives are, plus they keep you feeling full for longer – helping you to manage cravings and reset your relationship with food.

FRESH STAPLES

When it comes to fresh staples, I like to make a weekly batch of homemade almond, hemp or coconut milk (see page 21). These plant milks are a great addition to smoothies, soups or your morning coffee. When shopping for fresh ingredients, always go for a variety of fruits and vegetables, with varying colours, because as they say, it's best to eat the rainbow for an abundance of nutrients and for optimal gut health. Shop local and buy organic if you can – you will be supporting the right farming practices, without the use of pesticides and herbicides. If you are unable to source all organic, check out the Clean 15 and Dirty Dozen lists that are released each year. Put together by the Environmental Working Group (EWG), these lists detail the fruits and vegetables that contain the highest concentrations of pesticides – which the EWG recommends buying organic – as well as the 15 fruits and vegetables that contain the lowest concentrations of pesticides, which the EWG believes are the safest foods to buy conventionally, helping you strike a balance between what you can access and afford.

FROZEN STAPLES

Have you ever arrived home from a busy day and wished you had something you could just heat and eat? Well, if you cook in bulk you'll never go hungry again, as you'll always have ready-made meals on hand for those times when life happens. Stocking your freezer with lots of leftovers, offcuts and almost 'off' fruits and vegetables can be a game changer when it comes to saving both time and money. Creating smoothie bags and vegetable soup bags is a great idea too, as you can just blitz and drink or heat and eat – simply place your diced fruit and veggie leftovers and trimmings into sealable bags and freeze to use at a later date. Thinking twice about what you save and re-use is not only great for your pocket but also the environment (and if there is anything we should all be doing collectively, it is cutting down on waste).

HERBS

Herbs really bring food to life in so many ways. Beyond their vibrant colours and intense flavours, herbs also have many medicinal benefits. Some herbs even have unique healing nutrients that help balance, restore and protect the body. If you have any leftover fresh herbs, lay them out on baking paper in a warm part of the kitchen until dried and crisp, then store them in jars whole or crushed to use in future cooking. It's easy to stick to basil and parsley, but think outside the box and experiment with marjoram, lemon thyme and Vietnamese mint. My recipes alternate between fresh and dried herbs – just use what you have access to.

MUSHROOMS

I've given mushrooms their own special mention here as they are almost their own food group in the way that they contain certain health properties that cannot be found anywhere else. This includes, in particular, the different strains of bacteria they contain, which are beneficial for their positive contribution to good gut health, as well as their immunity-boosting properties. Cordyceps mushrooms in particular have been noted for their positive impact on cortisol levels and oxidative stress – it's for this reason that I add powdered mushrooms to my morning coffee (see page 18).

NUTS AND SEEDS

Nuts and seeds are a very important part of my plant-based approach. They add fantastic texture to a wide range of recipes, providing crunch and bite, and are also packed full of good-quality fats and protein, making them an excellent nutrient-dense source of energy. When it comes to nuts, I have a few favourites due to their fatty acid ratios, and these include macadamias, hazelnuts, walnuts and pecans. As for seeds, you can't go past hemp for nutrient density – these seeds are a complete source of protein, meaning they provide the body with all nine of the essential amino acids it needs (and cannot make on its own) to produce the building blocks for protein. Given relatively few plant-based foods are complete sources of protein, this makes hemp seeds a really valuable addition to a vegan diet.

OILS

Educating both vegans and non-vegans about healthy cooking oils is a great passion of mine, as I see lots of misinformation out there about what is best for our health. First and foremost, the oils we choose to cook with should be heat stable, non-hydrogenated, anti-inflammatory and retain their nutritional profile for nutrient density. Typical vegetable oils are some of the unhealthiest oils you can consume. They are often rich in hydrogenated, oxidised trans fats and can cause an inflammatory response due to their high omega-6 content and out-of-whack omega-6 to omega-3 ratio. So please avoid soybean oil, corn oil, cottonseed oil, grapeseed oil, canola oil and generic vegetable oils. Instead stick to heart healthy, nutrient-dense plant-based oils that can be cold pressed, meaning the oils are naturally occurring. Healthy, plant-based, cold-pressed oils include coconut oil, avocado oil, macadamia oil, hemp seed oil and extra-virgin olive oil. (This also goes for any vegan products like meat substitutes and cheeses that you might purchase – be sure to read packets carefully and stick to real food made on a farm, not in a lab.)

SPICES

Spices are truly your best friends in the kitchen, especially when it comes to plant-based cooking. They can take simple, everyday produce to the next level by adding a layer of complexity to the flavour – along with many additional health benefits, of course – making each meal a joy to eat. And, contrary to popular opinion, kids can manage various spices in their food. It's great to introduce small amounts of spice to children early on, to help mature their palates, as well as stimulate metabolism and immunity. We always hear about the benefits of turmeric, but don't forget the more 'everyday' spices such as chilli, which can help fight inflammation, boost immunity and act as natural pain relief. My recipes alternate between fresh and dried spices – just use whatever you have access to.

SWEETENERS

Once you've stocked your pantry with raw cacao in all its delicious forms, it seems only fitting that we talk about how we sweeten foods like raw chocolate. I love to help people reduce cravings and avoid overeating, and my goal is to get you to become an intuitive eater, in-tune with your body, eating when you're hungry and stopping when you're full. That means choosing sweeteners that put you in the driver's seat by helping you manage your blood-sugar levels. That is why I suggest sweeteners such as green leaf stevia, liquid stevia and monk fruit syrup for people who are following a low-carb approach, or real maple syrup and coconut nectar for a more moderate carb approach.

Sweeteners vary in flavour and consistency, so it's important to work out which one is right for you. For those following a low-carb keto approach, stevia is a great option. Green leaf stevia can be a little 'earthy' in flavour for some, so use it mindfully. Monk fruit syrup is one of my favourite sweeteners on the market and it's fantastic for those following a low-carb diet – if you can get your hands on the Lakanto brand, I really recommend it.

I love both maple syrup and coconut nectar and they work perfectly with most of my desserts. That said, they're not low-carb or keto friendly in higher amounts, so just be mindful of how much you consume if you're following a low-carb, healthy fat approach.

MORNINGS

The ULTIMATE
PLANT-BASED SMOOTHIE

We all know that greens are good for us, but eating enough on a daily basis can be a real struggle. This smoothie is a great way to get a real hit of your daily dose in a way that is quick and easy. Leafy greens supply our bodies with phytonutrients, antioxidants and many essential vitamins and minerals, and this smoothie offers up a delightful way of rapidly downing them along with plenty of other goodness. Try it – your tastebuds will thank you.

SERVES 1

125 ml (½ cup) almond, hemp or coconut milk, plus extra if needed
1 large handful of baby spinach or kale leaves, or 1 tablespoon powdered greens blend
1 kiwifruit, peeled
½ green apple, cored and deseeded
80 g (½ cup) fresh or frozen blueberries, plus extra to serve
1 tablespoon hemp seeds
1 tablespoon macadamia nuts
juice of ½ lemon
70 g (½ cup) ice

Put all the ingredients in a food processor and blitz on high to your preferred consistency (if it's a bit thick for your liking, loosen it up with some more milk). Pour into a glass, top with extra blueberries and enjoy as the perfect start to the day.

HEALTH TIP *Going low-carb or keto? Try swapping the green apple and kiwi for ½ ripe avocado. It will lower the overall carb content and increase the healthy omega-3 fats.*

TIP *They say you should be able to eat your smoothie like a meal. I think the chunkier the better. The more real food ingredients that give it texture and body, the more nutrients you will be getting. So, use a spoon to 'drink' it if need be! The good thing about this green smoothie is that, as with most of my smoothie recipes, it is highly customisable. Mix and match with what you've got on hand to make it to your liking.*

SALTED CHOCOLATE THICKSHAKE

If you're looking for a frying pan–free low-carb keto breakfast idea, this is definitely the place to start! Packed with healthy fats and plenty of nutrients, this refreshing dairy-free shake is an ideal way to start your day. The key when adding water here is to only use enough to get you to your preferred thickness – this is a 'thick' shake, after all, so add at your discretion.

SERVES 1

125 ml (½ cup) coconut milk or coconut cream
½ ripe avocado
2 tablespoons cacao powder
1 teaspoon MCT oil
½ teaspoon vanilla bean paste or powder
generous pinch of pink Himalayan salt, plus extra to serve
1 tablespoon monk fruit syrup or ¼ teaspoon green leaf stevia
70 g (½ cup) ice filtered water, as needed
cacao nibs, to serve

Put all the ingredients except the ice and water in a food processor and blitz until combined, then add your ice and a little water and blend to your preferred consistency. Do not over-blend, or the thickshake won't be as thick or cold. Pour into a glass, top with a few cacao nibs and a little extra salt and enjoy right away.

TIP *If you're not going low-carb or keto, you can swap out the monk fruit syrup or green leaf stevia for maple syrup or coconut nectar.*

HEALTH TIP *MCT oil is a very strong and pure blend of medium-chain triglycerides with no additives or fillers, just pure C8 and C10, creating the perfect combination of healthy fats for optimal performance. Derived from organic cold-pressed coconut oil, it is pure, clean and has no taste, making it perfect to add to any dish or drink.*

PUMPED-UP PUMPY SPICE LATTE

This ticks all the boxes when it comes to warmth, comfort and nourishment from the inside out. While it's typically a more wintery drink, you can make a cold version of this by blitzing it with some ice cubes and downing it as a yummy smoothie.

SERVES 1

200 ml almond, hemp or
  coconut milk
50 g pumpkin puree (see below)
⅛ teaspoon ground cinnamon
⅛ teaspoon ground ginger
⅛ teaspoon mixed spice
⅛ teaspoon ground turmeric
2 teaspoons maple syrup or
  1–2 drops liquid stevia
60 ml (¼ cup/2 shots) espresso
  coffee or 125 ml (½ cup)
  filter coffee

PUMPKIN PUREE (MAKES 500 G)
700 g butternut pumpkin, peeled
  and cut into 2.5 cm cubes

To make the pumpkin puree, add the pumpkin pieces to a large saucepan of boiling water and cook for 15–20 minutes, or until very tender when pressed with a fork. Drain and leave to cool, then transfer to a food processor or high-speed blender and blend to a puree.

In a small saucepan over medium heat whisk together the milk, 3 tablespoons of the pumpkin puree, the spices and sweetener of choice for 5–6 minutes, or until the mixture starts to bubble gently.

Transfer to a food processor, add your coffee and blitz until thick and frothy. (This can also be done with a hand-held blender or milk frother if you prefer.) Pour into your favourite mug and enjoy.

TIP *The pumpkin puree is a great one to make in bulk, as it can be used in many other recipes, including my Ultimate Chocolate Mousse (see page 160). Store leftover puree in an airtight container and keep it in the fridge for up to 3 days, or frozen for 3 months.*

HEALTH TIP *Pumpkin is often mistaken for a higher-carb root vegetable. The good news is that this above-ground vegetable is not only low-carb but is also packed with heaps of beneficial fibre.*

Magic Mushroom LATTE

Mushrooms are such nutrient powerhouses, they almost deserve their very own food group status, so it is no surprise that you can now access medicinal mushroom powders from health food stores. Here is how I enjoy my mushrooms for that magic feeling.

SERVES 2

250 ml (1 cup) almond, hemp or
  coconut milk
1 teaspoon powdered mushroom
  blend (see Health Tip)
30 ml (1 shot) espresso coffee
1 teaspoon MCT oil
¼ teaspoon vanilla bean paste
  or powder
1–2 drops liquid stevia (optional)

Add all the ingredients to a small saucepan over medium heat and whisk to combine. Continue to whisk until the mixture is heated, then transfer to a high-speed blender and blitz until thick and creamy. Pour into your favourite mug and enjoy.

TIP *If you like, omit the milk and instead of using an espresso shot, use a cup of brewed coffee or a large long black. Simply place all the ingredients into the blender and skip the saucepan warming.*

HEALTH TIP *When sourcing mushroom powders, look for pure blends that don't have any sweeteners or flavours added to them. The common ones to look for are reishi, shiitake and lion's mane.*

Pumped-up
pumpy spice latte

The ultimate Aztec
hot chocolate and cream
(see page 20)

Magic mushroom
latte

Vegan powerup
MCT coffee (see page 20)

VEGAN POWERUP MCT COFFEE

This recipe is the vegan take on my original PowerUP classic! Just a few simple ingredients combine to create the smoothest and most luxurious hit of energy and focus. The MCT oil in this drink provides your body with an easy-to-use source of energy, while the coconut butter delivers healthy fat, which, when combined with the coffee, creates a slow, sustained and epic fuel for your day.

I usually drink this unsweetened as I like a strong coffee flavour to start my day, but adding a dash of vanilla bean powder or a few drops of liquid stevia can be very helpful when it comes to curbing any sweet cravings I might be having.

SERVES 1

250 ml (1 cup) freshly brewed coffee
1 teaspoon–1 tablespoon MCT oil (see Health Tip, page 16)
1 tablespoon coconut butter vanilla bean powder or liquid stevia, to taste (optional)

Put all the ingredients in a food processor and blitz until well combined and frothy. Pour into your favourite mug, glass or re-usable coffee cup and enjoy.

TIP *When you're just starting out using MCT oil, it is best to introduce it slowly. Start with 1 teaspoon per drink and build your way up to 1 tablespoon. It has a very powerful effect on the body, so be sure to listen to yours and adjust the quantity accordingly.*

The ULTIMATE AZTEC HOT CHOCOLATE and CREAM

Hot chocolate's history goes quite a way back, and the drink has changed over the years, evolving from cold and spicy to warm and sweet. It all started in Mexico, as early as 500 BC, with the Mayans drinking chocolate made from ground cocoa seeds mixed with cold water, cornmeal and chilli peppers – very different to the version we know today. My recipe pays homage to the original with a hint of chilli, but brings things up to modern tastebuds' expectations by keeping it hot and adding a little sweetness in there for good measure.

SERVES 1

250 ml (1 cup) almond, hemp or coconut milk
1 tablespoon cacao powder, plus extra to serve
½ tablespoon maple syrup or 2–3 drops liquid stevia
⅛ teaspoon cayenne pepper, plus a pinch to serve
¼ teaspoon ground cinnamon
¼ teaspoon vanilla bean paste or powder
2 tablespoons boiling water (optional)
1 tablespoon coconut cream
½ teaspoon cacao nibs

Add the milk, cacao powder, maple syrup or stevia, cayenne pepper, cinnamon and vanilla to a saucepan set over medium–low heat. Whisk until well combined and beginning to simmer.

Transfer the mixture to a food processor and blitz until thick and creamy (add a little boiling water when you're blending if it's too thick for your liking). Pour into a large mug, top with the coconut cream and cacao nibs and sprinkle over a little extra cacao powder to finish.

TIP *I always keep a can of coconut cream in my fridge upside down. This allows the thick fattier components to settle at the top when I open it – perfect for scooping out for a thick dollop of the delicious stuff.*

HOMEMADE PLANT MILKS

Making your own plant-based milks is a game changer when it comes to flavour and nutrition. By using the simple ingredients listed below, you can avoid the processed and refined vegetable oils, sugars and thickening agents that some store-bought plant milks contain.

Hemp Milk

MAKES 1.25 LITRES (5 CUPS)

170 g (1 cup) shelled hemp seeds
750 ml (3 cups) filtered water
pinch of sea salt

Combine the hemp seeds, water and salt in a blender or food processor. Blitz on high for 30–60 seconds, until the seeds are completely pulverised.

For maximum nutrition, leave the milk unstrained, or strain for a smoother milk to use in recipes. Line a bowl with either a nut milk bag or a piece of muslin, so that the fabric hangs over the edge of the bowl. Pour the hemp milk into the bowl, then pick up the edges of the bag or muslin and squeeze out as much liquid as possible.

Store the milk in a sealed container in the fridge for up to 3 days.

Almond Milk

MAKES 1.25 LITRES (5 CUPS)

155 g (1 cup) raw almonds, soaked
in water for at least 8 hours
1 litre (4 cups) filtered water
1 vanilla pod, split and scraped
pinch of sea salt

Drain the soaked nuts and rinse them really well. Place all the ingredients in a high-speed blender and blend for 2–3 minutes, or until nice and creamy.

Line a bowl with either a nut milk bag or a piece of muslin, so that the fabric hangs over the edge of the bowl. Pour the blended nut and water mixture into the bowl. Pick up the edges of the bag or muslin and squeeze out all the milk (like milking the nuts, so to speak!). Keep the leftover pulp to use in your baking.

Store the milk in an airtight container in the fridge for up to 4 days, being sure to shake well before each use.

Coconut Milk

MAKES 1.25 LITRES (5 CUPS)

1 litre (4 cups) filtered water
120 g (2 cups) shredded coconut
1 vanilla pod, split and scraped
pinch of sea salt

Pour the filtered water into a saucepan over medium heat and bring to a simmer. Remove from the heat and pour into a high-speed blender. Add the coconut, vanilla seeds and salt and blend or pulse on high for 2–5 minutes, or until the liquid becomes thick and creamy.

Line a colander with two large layers of muslin and place over a large bowl. Pour the coconut milk into the lined colander, then pick up the edges of the muslin and squeeze as much liquid as possible out of the coconut through the colander into the bowl.

Store the coconut milk in an airtight container in the refrigerator for up to 3–4 days, being sure to give it a bit of a shake before use as the solids can settle on the bottom.

Blue Avocado BREAKFAST BOWL

Sincere apologies to all the toast lovers out there, but I am putting my smashed avocado into this yummy recipe instead. I love smoothie bowls and I love avocados for their epic nutritional content; the addition of blueberries really complements the richness the avocado brings to the table.

SERVES 1

155 g (1 cup) fresh or frozen blueberries
½ avocado
125 ml (½ cup) almond, hemp or coconut milk
1 tablespoon LSA (see Health Tip)
1 teaspoon maple syrup, coconut nectar or 1–2 drops liquid stevia
¼ teaspoon vanilla bean paste or powder
3–4 ice cubes

TOPPINGS
1 small handful of fresh blueberries
1 heaped tablespoon chopped Luke's Chocolate (see page 150)
1 teaspoon hemp seeds
½ teaspoon chia seeds

Add all the bowl ingredients to a high-speed blender and whiz together until smooth and creamy. Pour into a bowl and top with the blueberries, chopped chocolate, hemp and chia seeds. Enjoy immediately.

HEALTH TIP *LSA is made from ground flaxseeds (linseeds), sunflower seeds and almonds, and is an easy, extremely versatile way to add extra nutrients to meals. It's also rich in protein, which helps to keep your blood sugar levels balanced and curb any sugar cravings.*

BANOFFEE BREAKFAST BOWL

Banoffee pie is a classic English dessert in which bananas, cream and toffee are combined on a buttery biscuit base. Some versions also include chocolate or coffee (or both). Here I have put these flavours together to make this quick, easy and healthy smoothie bowl.

SERVES 1

125 ml (½ cup) almond, hemp or coconut milk
1 large frozen banana
1 tablespoon cacao powder
1 tablespoon peanut butter, plus extra for drizzling
2 tablespoons LSA (see Health Tip, above)
60 ml (¼ cup/2 shots) espresso coffee, cooled
1 teaspoon maple syrup, coconut nectar or 1–2 drops liquid stevia (optional)

TOPPINGS
½ teaspoon cacao nibs
½ teaspoon roasted coffee beans, roughly chopped
½ small banana, sliced

Add the milk, frozen banana, cacao powder, peanut butter, LSA, coffee and sweetener, if using, to a high-speed blender and blitz together to combine. Pour into a bowl and top with the cacao nibs, coffee beans, sliced banana and an extra drizzle of peanut butter, if you like. Enjoy.

HEALTH TIP *The key to having a healthy relationship with coffee is making sure you don't drink too much of it! Keep your daily limit to two shots in whatever way you like to enjoy it. Caffeine is a powerful stimulant but, if overconsumed, can harm our adrenals – making us feel tired and lethargic. I also recommend you embrace organic coffee as coffee beans are one of the crops most heavily sprayed with harmful pesticides. Keep it clean, guys.*

GREEN APPLE *and* LIME
HEMP BIRCHER

Hemp seeds come from the heart of the hemp plant and I just adore using them for all types of recipes, from making your own hemp milk to this hemp bircher. Creamy and delicious, this needs to be started the day before, making it perfect for when you do your meal prep.

In the pantry section (see page 11) I touched on how important it is to have a good omega-6 to omega-3 ratio, and hemp seeds come in on top with healthy fatty acids that are anti-inflammatory and promote cardiovascular health. Plus, they are the most wonderful source of protein for vegans. They are known as a 'complete' protein source as they provide all nine essential amino acids, which are the building blocks of protein that our bodies cannot produce so have to absorb through diet.

SERVES 2

85 g (½ cup) hemp seeds, plus extra to serve

2 tablespoons chia seeds

1 tablespoon flaxseeds

½ teaspoon vanilla bean paste or powder

½ teaspoon ground cinnamon

125 g (½ cup) coconut yoghurt or chilled coconut cream, plus extra to serve

185 ml (¾ cup) almond, hemp or coconut milk

1 green apple, grated, plus extra sliced apple to serve

zest and juice of 1 lime

1 tablespoon pistachio slivers

50 g (⅓ cup) fresh blueberries

1 tablespoon maple syrup or coconut nectar

Place the hemp seeds, chia seeds, flaxseeds, vanilla, cinnamon, coconut yoghurt or cream and milk in a bowl and mix well to combine. Cover and place in the fridge overnight.

When ready to serve, stir through the grated apple, lime zest and juice, and divide between two bowls. Top with an extra dollop of coconut yoghurt or cream, the apple slices, pistachio slivers, blueberries and a drizzle of your preferred sweetener.

HEALTH TIP *A hemp seed is like a little nut with a crisp shell and a soft heart. Up until mid 2017 they were actually restricted from being sold in Australia, though now you can find them for sale in health food shops as well as some supermarkets. Typically, you will find the hearts for sale – already released from their shells – and these have a mild, nutty flavour. In order to be considered a food ingredient in this country, hemp seeds have to contain less than 0.5% of the psychoactive ingredient tetrahydrocannabinol (THC) and are therefore referred to as low-THC hemp.*

BANANA *and* PEANUT BUTTER BREAKFAST COOKIES

There is so much to love about these beauties! These devourable little cookies make a great change from the usual breakfast granolas or smoothies, though they are still packed with healthy staples like bananas, walnuts and almonds. The best news is that all you need to do is throw everything into one bowl, then mix, bake and eat. They will keep for several days in an airtight container, so you can make a big batch on a Sunday arvo and grab a couple on your way out the door every day of the week. Cookies for breakfast all week long? That's a win in my eyes.

MAKES 12

2 bananas, sliced

125 g (½ cup) chunky peanut butter

3 tablespoons filtered water

1 teaspoon vanilla bean paste or powder

100 g (1 cup) almond meal

1 teaspoon gluten-free baking powder

1 teaspoon ground cinnamon

½ teaspoon sea salt

3 tablespoons cacao nibs or roughly chopped homemade healthy chocolate (see Tip)

3 tablespoons shredded coconut

3 tablespoons roughly chopped pecans or walnuts

3 tablespoons roughly chopped macadamia nuts

smooth peanut butter, for drizzling (optional)

Preheat the oven to 180°C and line a baking tray with baking paper.

Add the banana, peanut butter, water and vanilla to a large bowl and beat with an electric whisk or whiz with a hand-held blender until mostly smooth. Add in the almond meal, baking powder, cinnamon and salt and beat again until really well combined. Using a spoon, gently fold in the cacao nibs or chopped chocolate, shredded coconut and nuts.

Dollop the sticky dough into 12 equal mounds on the prepared trays. Place in the oven and bake for 15–18 minutes, or until the bottoms are firm and the edges are golden.

Remove the cookies from the oven and leave them to cool slightly on the tray. Drizzle over the smooth peanut butter (if using) and enjoy.

TIP *I love cacao nibs as they are an easy, healthy alternative to regular chocolate chips, but if you've got time, making some easy homemade chocolate and using that as the chips is even better as it creates a lovely melted chocolate effect. See page 150 for details of how to make a slab of raw chocolate, which you can chop roughly and use in place of the nibs.*

CHOCOLATE 'GET YOUR GREENS' AVO BICKIES

Not a fan of green smoothies or salads for breakfast? No worries! These delicious, easy-to-make bickies will help you start your day with a good dose of greens. I've recommended using finely chopped baby spinach here, but you can swap that for any other leafy greens you've got in the house.

MAKES 20

½ large avocado

1 banana

1 large handful of baby spinach or kale leaves, finely chopped

60 g (½ cup) cacao powder

3 tablespoons maple syrup, coconut nectar or monk fruit syrup

150 g (1½ cups) almond meal or hemp flour

3 tablespoons coconut flour

1 tablespoon chia seeds

1 teaspoon ground cinnamon

½ teaspoon vanilla bean paste or powder

1 teaspoon gluten-free baking powder

generous pinch of sea salt

melted Luke's Chocolate (see page 150), for drizzling (optional)

Preheat the oven to 180°C and line two baking trays with baking paper.

Place the avocado and banana in a bowl and use the back of a fork to mash them together until smooth. Add in the remaining ingredients and mix everything together until evenly combined.

Transfer the bowl to the fridge so the chia seeds can get to work expanding, firming up and binding your mix. This should take about 20 minutes.

Once ready to cook, use your hands to roll a heaped tablespoon of the dough into a ball. Press it down on the tray to flatten it slightly, then repeat with the rest of the dough. Bake for 20 minutes, or until the bickies are golden brown on the outside.

Remove from the oven and leave to cool slightly on the trays. Drizzle over the melted chocolate (if using) and enjoy.

The bickies can be stored in an airtight container for up to 4 days or frozen for 3 months.

TIP *When it comes to using vanilla, try to source a 100 per cent vanilla bean paste or powder from your local health food store or online retailer or use seeds scraped from the pod (in which case use 1 vanilla pod for every ½ teaspoon of paste or powder). The real taste of pure vanilla beats the liquids and essences any day.*

HEALTH TIP *Avocados truly are a superfood. Containing more potassium than bananas, they are loaded with heart-healthy monounsaturated fatty acids in the form of oleic acid, which is also the major component of olive oil and believed to be responsible for some of its health benefits. The fats in avocado are also resistant to oxidation at high temperatures, which means avocado oil is a great choice for cooking.*

Chocolate
'get your greens'
avo bickies
(see page 27)

Banana and peanut butter
breakfast cookies (see page 26)

BANGIN' BANANA *and* WALNUT BREAD

Banana bread is statistically the most sought-after bread in online searches and for very good reason – it's absolutely delicious! This version is free of refined sugars, inflammatory oils and contains real bananas. So, ditch that store-bought version for one that is easier to make than ever. Please note that adding the sweetener to this recipe is optional, as very ripe bananas are already sweet enough (like you).

MAKES 1 LOAF

125 ml (½ cup) melted coconut oil
2 large overripe bananas, mashed
2 Flax Eggs (see recipe below)
2 tablespoons maple syrup
   or coconut nectar (optional
   if you like a sweeter bread)
1 teaspoon vanilla bean paste
   or powder
200 g (2 cups) almond meal
100 g (1 cup) walnuts, roughly
   crushed, plus extra for
   sprinkling
1 teaspoon gluten-free baking
   powder
1 teaspoon ground cinnamon
¼ teaspoon sea salt
Vegan Butter (see page 32),
   to serve (optional)

Preheat the oven to 180°C and line a 22 cm loaf tin with baking paper.

In a large bowl, combine the melted coconut oil, mashed banana, flax eggs and sweetener, if using, and whisk together until well combined.

In a separate bowl, combine the dry ingredients and mix well.

Combine the wet and dry mixtures and mix well. Pour into the prepared loaf tin and bake for 55 minutes, or until golden brown on top and a toothpick inserted in the centre comes out clean.

Remove the bread from the oven and leave to cool slightly, then remove from the tin, transfer to a wire rack and leave to cool completely. Slice and serve with some vegan butter, if you like. The loaf will keep for up to 4 days in the fridge and for up to 3 months in the freezer (I like to pre-slice it so that it's easy to take one piece out at a time).

HOW TO MAKE FLAX EGGS

To make a flax egg, mix 1½ tablespoons of flaxseed meal with 3 tablespoons of water in a bowl. Transfer to the fridge and leave for 15–30 minutes, or until the mixture has begun to bind and thicken and is all 'goopy', like an egg. It's as simple as that. For more flax eggs, just scale up the quantities (for two flax eggs, double them, and so on). And if you don't like flaxseeds? Simply substitute the ground flax out for the same quantity of ground chia seeds. Too easy.

HEALTH TIP *Walnuts are an excellent source of antioxidants that can help fight oxidative damage in your body, including damage caused by 'bad' LDL cholesterol. Also, several of the plant compounds and nutrients in walnuts may help decrease inflammation, which is a key culprit in many chronic diseases.*

SAVOURY HEMP BREAD *with* VEGAN BUTTER *and* VEGANMITE

Let me introduce you to buckwheat. This gluten-free superfood is a seed rather than a grain, has a low glycaemic index (so will help you manage your blood-sugar levels) and is packed with protein, fibre, B vitamins and minerals, as well as possessing anti-inflammatory properties that will keep you feeling full for longer. Ground into a flour, you can find it at most health food stores as well as major supermarkets, and it works especially well for baking muffins, crepes, pancakes and, of course, breads like this one. This recipe is best served toasted with a generous smear of my vegan butter and a good slathering of my gluten-free take on the Aussie classic Vegemite.

MAKES 1 LOAF

150 g (1½ cups) almond meal
140 g (1 cup) buckwheat flour
3 tablespoons psyllium husks
3 tablespoons chia seeds
255 g (1½ cups) hemp seeds
2 teaspoons bicarbonate of soda
½ teaspoon sea salt
500 ml (2 cups) filtered water
2 tablespoons maple syrup or
    coconut nectar
2 tablespoons apple cider vinegar

VEGAN BUTTER (MAKES 250 G)
125 ml (½ cup) coconut oil
125 ml (½ cup) extra-virgin olive
    or avocado oil
2 tablespoons coconut cream
½ teaspoon sea salt
pinch of ground turmeric

VEGANMITE (MAKES 300 G)
125 ml (½ cup) black tahini
2 tablespoons coconut aminos
1 tablespoon nutritional yeast
    flakes
1 teaspoon apple cider vinegar
¼ teaspoon onion powder
¼ teaspoon garlic powder

For the vegan butter, blitz all the ingredients in a high-speed blender until smooth and creamy. Pour into a suitable container, seal with a lid and refrigerate for 3–4 hours, or until set. Store in the fridge for up to 2 weeks.

To make the veganmite, put all the ingredients in a food processor or high-speed blender and blitz until well combined. Transfer to an airtight container and store in the fridge for up to 4 weeks.

Combine the almond meal, buckwheat flour, psyllium, chia, hemp, bicarb and salt in a large bowl. Stir well to make sure there are no lumps in the mix and everything is evenly distributed.

In a separate smaller bowl, whisk together the water, sweetener and apple cider vinegar to combine.

Pour the wet mix into the dry mix and stir to combine. Cover with a tea towel and leave to sit in the bowl at room temperature for about 1 hour.

Preheat the oven to 180°C and line a 22 cm loaf tin with baking paper.

Once your 'dough' is feeling sticky and has absorbed any excess water, scoop it into your prepared loaf tin and smooth the top out evenly. (I like to give it a gentle bang down onto a chopping board on the bench to even things out and remove any air bubbles.) Bake for 1 hour, or until the loaf is dark brown on top and firm to touch. Remove from the oven and leave to cool slightly, then turn out onto a wire rack and leave to cool completely. Once cooled, slice the loaf and keep in the fridge for up to 1 week or in the freezer for up to 3 months.

To serve, toast the savoury hemp bread slices, then spread generously with the vegan butter followed by a thick layer of veganmite. Perfection.

TIP *Black tahini is now available in most good health food stores. It is made from black sesame seeds that are stone ground and is very similar in taste to hulled white tahini, though its greyish black colour makes it perfect for this recipe.*

One bowl
BREAKFAST MUFFINS

Anything 'one bowl' is the best, because it means less mess in the kitchen and more time to spend enjoying the delicious creations you make. That said, my favourite thing about these muffins is the abundance of nutrient-rich fruit and veg that's packed into them. They're done in no time at all and are an absolute joy to eat.

MAKES 12

2 Flax Eggs (see page 31)
120 g (½ cup) mashed very ripe banana
3 tablespoons maple syrup, coconut nectar or monk fruit syrup
3 tablespoons extra-virgin olive oil, plus extra for greasing
125 g (½ cup) finely grated green apple
70 g (½ cup) coconut sugar
1½ teaspoons gluten-free baking powder
½ teaspoon sea salt
½ teaspoon ground cinnamon
125 ml (½ cup) almond, hemp or coconut milk
155 g (1 cup) grated carrot (about 2 small carrots)
135 g (1 cup) grated zucchini (about 1 zucchini), squeezed of excess liquid
170 g (1 cup) hemp seeds
200 g (2 cups) almond meal
3 tablespoons roughly chopped walnuts, to serve

Preheat the oven to 190°C and grease a 12-hole muffin tin with oil or line it with paper cases.

Prepare your flax eggs in a large bowl so they have time to thicken. Once the flax eggs are thick and goopy, add in the mashed banana, sweetener and olive oil and whisk well to combine, then add all the remaining ingredients except the walnuts and stir to form a batter.

Spoon the batter evenly into the prepared muffin tin, scatter over the walnuts and bake for 40–45 minutes, or until the muffins are lovely and golden brown on top, firm when pressed and a toothpick inserted in the centre comes out clean. (When you press on the top it shouldn't feel too spongey, so don't be afraid of baking these for a little longer if need be to cook them through.)

Turn the muffins out onto a wire rack to cool. Enjoy straight away or store in an airtight container in the fridge for up to 5 days or freeze for up to 3 months.

TIP *This is a great recipe to cook up in large batches so that you have extras in the fridge and freezer. Containing fruits, vegetables and healthy fats, these muffins will keep you feeling full and are a meal in themselves, making them perfect for those busy mornings when you're running out the door.*

SPICY SWEET POTATO ROSTIS
with INDIAN AVO SMASH

I love all things crispy and spicy, which makes this quick and easy recipe a real winner for me. As a change from the regular smashed avocado or Mexican-flavoured guacamole, I think you are going to love this Indian-inspired take on the yummy favourite. It's deliciously zesty and really brings out the flavours in the rostis themselves.

SERVES 4

350 g sweet potato (about 2), peeled and grated
2 Flax Eggs (see page 31)
¼ cup chopped coriander leaves
½ teaspoon chilli flakes (optional)
sea salt and freshly ground black pepper
2 tablespoons coconut oil

INDIAN AVO SMASH

1 large avocado, roughly mashed
1 tablespoon chopped coriander leaves, plus extra to serve
¼ red onion, finely diced
½ teaspoon ground cumin
½ teaspoon ground coriander
½ teaspoon chilli flakes, plus extra to serve
zest and juice of 1 lime, plus extra wedges to serve
2 tablespoons extra-virgin olive oil (optional)
1 tablespoon apple cider vinegar (optional)
sea salt and freshly ground black pepper

For the avo smash, add all the ingredients to a bowl and mash them together with a fork (I sometimes add a little more extra-virgin olive oil and apple cider vinegar to this if the avocado is a bit firm). Season well with salt and pepper and set aside.

Add the sweet potato, flax eggs, chopped coriander and chilli flakes to a bowl, season with salt and pepper and mix well to combine.

Heat 1 tablespoon of the coconut oil in a large non-stick frying pan over medium heat. Working in batches, ladle 3 tablespoons of the sweet potato mixture per rosti into the pan and spread it out a little, then cook for 3–4 minutes, or until golden and crispy and firm enough to flip with a spatula. Turn and cook for a further 3–4 minutes, then drain on paper towel and transfer to a low oven to keep warm while you cook the rest, adding the remaining coconut oil to the pan as you go.

When ready to serve, divide the rostis among plates, top with the spiced avo smash and scatter over the extra coriander leaves, chilli flakes and an extra sprinkling of salt. Enjoy with the lime wedges on the side for squeezing over.

HEALTH TIP *If you're looking to lose excess body fat, managing your consumption of sugars, starches and other carbs can help your progress. A new term being thrown around a lot lately is a type of carb called 'resistant starch'. Resistant starch isn't completely broken down and absorbed by the body, but rather is turned into short-chain fatty acids by intestinal bacteria. Studies show that resistant starch can actually boost weight loss by regulating insulin, promoting gut health, and helping you feel fuller longer. Sweet potato is a fantastic ingredient to use to create a healthy form of resistant starch.*

ROASTED HEMP *and* MACADAMIA MUSHROOMS

Stuffed mushrooms are one of the easiest and most delicious meals you can put together. A great start to the day or a fuss-free lunch, this recipe is a celebration of simple flavours that go really well together on the plate. For those new to hemp, this is a fantastic way to incorporate the seeds into your meals – they add a punch of nutty flavour, along with all the health benefits that go with them too, of course.

SERVES 4

8 large portobello mushrooms, stalks removed and reserved
2 garlic cloves, very finely chopped
3 tablespoons hemp seeds
3 tablespoons crushed macadamia nuts, plus 2 tablespoons toasted and roughly chopped macadamias to serve
zest and juice of 1 lemon, plus extra zest to serve
½ teaspoon sea salt
100 ml extra-virgin olive or avocado oil
1 bunch of flat-leaf parsley, leaves roughly chopped
freshly ground black pepper

Preheat the oven to 200°C and line a baking tray with baking paper.

Add the mushroom stalks, garlic, hemp seeds, crushed macadamia nuts, lemon zest and juice, salt and 3 tablespoons of the oil to a food processor along with the parsley, reserving a tablespoon or so for garnish. Pulse briefly to form a rough, wet paste.

Arrange the mushrooms, gill-side up, on the prepared tray and spoon over the paste mixture. Drizzle over the remaining oil and bake for 20–25 minutes, or until the mushrooms are soft and cooked through and the herb crust is golden brown.

Divide the baked mushrooms among plates, season with salt and pepper and serve topped with the chopped toasted macadamias, a little extra lemon zest and the reserved chopped parsley.

HEALTH TIP *The amount of omega-3s in hemp seeds and the seeds' healthful omega-3 to omega-6 ratio can help to reduce inflammation. In addition, hemp seeds are a rich source of gamma linolenic acid (GLA), a polyunsaturated fatty acid which may also have anti-inflammatory effects. Great news on all fronts!*

CHARRED PUMPKIN BREAKFAST TORTILLAS

It doesn't get much simpler or more delicious than this dish. You get to create a fantastic gluten-free crispy tortilla from scratch and, while you're doing that, you're also roasting off possibly one of my favourite vegetables, the humble butternut pumpkin. This naturally sweet and delicious vegetable is low-carb, packed with nutrients and just makes you feel good inside.

SERVES 4

400 g butternut pumpkin, unpeeled, roughly diced into small chunks
2 tablespoons coconut oil
½ teaspoon sea salt
2 tablespoons sesame seeds, lightly toasted
lemon wedges, to serve

CRISPY TORTILLAS
100 g (1 cup) almond meal
125 g (1 cup) arrowroot or tapioca flour
125 ml (½ cup) coconut milk
125 ml (½ cup) filtered water, plus extra if needed
½ teaspoon sea salt
3–4 tablespoons coconut oil

HERBY AVOCADO DRESSING
1 avocado, smashed
1 large handful of flat-leaf parsley leaves, roughly chopped
125 ml (½ cup) extra-virgin olive, avocado, macadamia or hemp oil
1 teaspoon apple cider vinegar
zest and juice of 1 lemon
½ teaspoon sea salt

Preheat the oven to 200°C and line a baking tray with baking paper.

Coat your pumpkin well with the coconut oil, season with the salt and spread evenly over your prepared baking tray, giving each chunk space to get crispy without too much overlapping. Bake for about 30 minutes, or until golden brown around the edges and soft in the middle.

While your pumpkin is cooking, get on with the tortillas. Combine the almond meal, arrowroot or tapioca flour, coconut milk, water and salt in a bowl and mix well to form a smooth thin batter. (The more watery the batter, the thinner and crispier your tortillas will be, so add a splash or two more if you like.) Melt 1 tablespoon of the coconut oil in a small non-stick frying pan over medium heat. Ladle a quarter of the batter into the pan, tilting and swirling it to coat the base in an even layer, and cook for 2–3 minutes, then carefully turn the tortilla over with a spatula and cook for a further 2 minutes, or until golden and cooked through. Lift the tortilla from the pan and set aside, wrapped in a clean tea towel to keep warm. Repeat with the remaining mixture, greasing the pan with a little more coconut oil in between tortillas to make sure they don't stick to the pan.

For the herby avocado dressing, put all the ingredients in a food processor and pulse until smooth and creamy.

Divide the tortillas among plates, spoon over the roasted pumpkin, drizzle with the dressing and sprinkle over the toasted sesame seeds. Serve with the lemon wedges and tuck in.

CAULIFLOWER *and* 'CHORIZO' SCRAMBLE *with* SPICY GREEN SAUCE

This plant-based chorizo mixture packs all the flavour and punch of its traditional counterpart along with all the vegan goodness of fresh produce. The recipe below is a great starting point, but feel free to adjust the spices if you like things hotter. When it comes to the cauliflower, be sure to cut it down into lovely small chunks to help it cook quicker and more evenly.

SERVES 4

1 tablespoon coconut oil
¼ teaspoon ground turmeric
1 head of cauliflower, roughly cut into 1 cm chunks
1 handful of baby rocket leaves
sea salt and freshly ground black pepper

CHORIZO SAUCE
1 long red chilli, deseeded and roughly chopped
1 teaspoon garlic powder
1 teaspoon onion powder
1 teaspoon smoked paprika
100 g (1 cup) pecans, toasted
150 g cherry tomatoes, chopped

SPICY GREEN SAUCE
125 ml (½ cup) extra-virgin olive, avocado, macadamia or hemp oil
4 spring onions, finely sliced
1 teaspoon ground cumin
1 teaspoon ground coriander
2 handfuls of coriander, stalks and leaves, roughly chopped
2 small red chillies, roughly chopped
zest and juice of 1 lime
1 tablespoon apple cider vinegar

For the chorizo sauce, add the chilli, garlic and onion powders, paprika and pecans to a food processor and pulse to combine. Transfer to a bowl, stir through the tomato and set aside.

For the spicy green sauce, rinse and wipe dry the food processor, then add all the ingredients and blitz until well combined. Set aside.

Heat the coconut oil and turmeric in a large frying pan over medium heat. Add the cauliflower and saute for 6–8 minutes, or until it begins to become golden brown around the edges and softens slightly. Add the prepared chorizo sauce and continue to saute until everything is fragrant and the cauliflower pieces are completely coated in the mixture.

Spoon the cauliflower and chorizo scramble into shallow bowls and add a generous drizzle of the green sauce. Add the rocket leaves, season well with salt and pepper and enjoy.

ZUCCHINI *and* HEMP HASH BROWNS *with* DREAM CHEESE

You know how I love creating healthier versions of everyday classics? Well, I am a massive fan of the original potato hash brown. But given these days I am gluten-free and low-carb, I had to get creative in the kitchen to make this beauty so that you and I can enjoy those same flavours and mouthfeel without any of the processed or high-carb nasties. If you want to take these to the next level, simply add some different herbs and spices and you're set! They're perfect for pairing with my take on cream cheese – 'dream cheese' – a 100 per cent vegan alternative that tastes better than the original.

SERVES 4 (ABOUT 12 FRITTERS)

2 zucchini
1 parsnip, grated
3 tablespoons hemp seeds
2 tablespoons coconut flour
1 tablespoon arrowroot or
    tapioca flour, plus extra
    if needed
½ teaspoon garlic powder
½ teaspoon onion powder
½ teaspoon sea salt
2 Flax Eggs (see page 31)
2 tablespoons coconut oil, plus
    extra if needed
freshly ground black pepper

DREAM CHEESE (MAKES 250 G)
200 g (1¼ cups) macadamia nuts
    or cashew nuts
3 tablespoons coconut milk or
    coconut cream
2 tablespoons apple cider vinegar
juice of ½ lemon
½ teaspoon sea salt

TO SERVE
lemon wedges
dill fronds
mint leaves

For the dream cheese, add all the ingredients to a food processor or high-speed blender and blitz until smooth and creamy. Set aside in the fridge until needed.

Grate the zucchini and place it on a clean tea towel or muslin cloth, then hold it over the sink and squeeze out the excess liquid for a couple of minutes until the zucchini is lovely and dry. Alternatively, place the grated zucchini in a colander and squeeze out the liquid over the sink.

Add the zucchini, grated parsnip, hemp seeds, coconut flour, arrowroot or tapioca flour, garlic and onion powders, salt and the flax eggs to a bowl and mix well to form a thick batter. If it is looking a little wet, simply add a touch more arrowroot or tapioca flour to help it come together.

Melt the coconut oil in a large non-stick frying pan over medium heat. Working in batches of about four at a time, dollop 2 tablespoons of mixture into the pan and use the back of your spoon or a spatula to shape it into a rectangle for that classic hash brown look. Cook for 3–4 minutes, or until the hash browns are golden brown on the underside and holding their form, then flip carefully with a spatula and continue to cook for a further 2–3 minutes, or until both sides are golden brown. Add extra coconut oil to the pan between batches if need be.

Season well with salt and pepper and serve immediately with the dream cheese, lemon wedges and herbs, or pack away into an airtight container or school lunchbox and store in the fridge for enjoying later.

TIP *Want to take your dream cheese to the next level? Try adding some different flavourings to your recipe. For a chive and onion dream cheese, simply blend in 1 teaspoon of onion powder with the other ingredients and stir in 4 tablespoons of chopped chives once smooth. And to give your cheese a really smooth finish, try soaking your nuts for 1 hour in hot water, then drain before blending.*

ROASTED BROCCOLI STEAKS
with GREEN TAHINI

Your weekend breakfast just went up a notch! Seriously, you won't be missing your local cafe feed once you cook up this beauty of a recipe. Super simple and packed with so much flavour, it is the best way to start your day. Feel free to mix it up and use cauliflower instead of broccoli, or swap the pine nuts for a spicy and zesty dukkah (see page 112).

SERVES 4

2 large heads of broccoli
1–2 tablespoons coconut oil
sea salt and freshly ground
   black pepper
1 tablespoon chilli flakes
2 tablespoons pine nuts, toasted
zest and juice of 1 lime (zest
   optional)

GREEN TAHINI
3 tablespoons hulled tahini
90 g (⅓ cup) coconut yoghurt or
   thick canned coconut cream
2 large handfuls of flat-leaf parsley
   leaves, roughly chopped
2 garlic cloves, roughly chopped
zest and juice of 1 lemon
2 tablespoons extra-virgin olive,
   avocado, macadamia or hemp oil
1 tablespoon apple-cider vinegar
1–2 tablespoons filtered water
   (optional)

Preheat the oven to 180°C and line a baking tray with baking paper.

Sit each broccoli head upright on your chopping board and cut two even slices, each about 2 cm thick, out of the centre.

Melt 1 tablespoon of the coconut oil in a frying pan over high heat. Add one of the broccoli steaks and fry for 4 minutes, turning halfway through, or until nicely golden brown and caramelised. Transfer the caramelised steak to the prepared baking tray and repeat with the remaining broccoli steaks, adding more coconut oil if need be.

Season the broccoli steaks well with salt and pepper and scatter over the chilli flakes, then roast in the oven for 20–30 minutes, or until cooked through and soft on the inside and golden brown on the edges.

Meanwhile, for the green tahini, place the ingredients in a food processor or high-speed blender and blitz until well combined. The sauce should be thick and creamy. Add a little water if you need to loosen it up.

To serve, spoon the green tahini onto serving plates, smearing to cover the bases well. Top with the charred broccoli steaks, sprinkle with the roughly chopped pine nuts and lime zest (if using) and finish with a generous squeeze of lime juice.

HEALTH TIP *Compared to other nuts and seeds, sesame seeds have one of the highest oil contents by weight (about 55 per cent), which is why tahini is exceptionally silky smooth and perfect for this recipe. It also contains around 20 per cent protein and a number of essential amino acids, meaning it stacks up very favourably against the likes of peanut butter and almond butter.*

CRISPY

— · and · —

CRUNCHY

MASSAGED KALE SALAD
with PLANT PARMESAN

Kale can sometimes get a bad rap as it can be quite coarse and a bit of a workout to eat in its raw state. Showing it a little love and tender care with a couple of minutes of massage, however, helps transform it into a really soft and tender salad you'll just love. Now, I realise it might sound odd to massage your greens, but if you haven't done it before you'll be shocked by the difference it makes. One thing I love about this salad is that you can make it, then refrigerate it and it will still be perfect the next day. It won't get wilted or soggy once it's been tossed with dressing, so it's the perfect salad to make ahead for lunch. Just add your favourite salad fixings on top and you're good to go.

SERVES 4

1 large bunch of kale (about 600 g), stalks removed and leaves cut into 5 mm thick ribbons

1 tablespoon extra-virgin olive or avocado oil

½ teaspoon sea salt

zest and juice of 2 lemons

3 tablespoons pepitas, toasted and finely chopped

PLANT PARMESAN (MAKES 140 G)

120 g (¾ cup) cashew nuts

25 g (⅓ cup) nutritional yeast flakes

¾ teaspoon sea salt

¼ teaspoon garlic powder

For the plant parmesan, pulse all the ingredients in a food processor until you have a fine meal similar to finely grated parmesan cheese.

Place the kale, oil and salt in a large bowl and, using your hands, massage the kale for 3–4 minutes, or until it softens and becomes lovely and tender.

Add the lemon zest and juice to the bowl together with the pepitas and toss to combine, then sprinkle over 70 g (½ cup) of the plant parmesan and serve. The leftover parmesan will keep in an airtight container in the fridge for up to 1 month.

HEALTH TIP *As well as being a rich source of important vitamins, minerals, protein and fibre, nutritional yeast is a plant-based ingredient that adds a pleasing yellow-orange colour, a cheesy, nutty flavour and a burst of umami to almost anything. It is a really useful alternative to dairy cheese in vegan dishes and can be found at most supermarkets and health food stores.*

The
COVER-WORTHY WELLNESS BOWL

When putting this book together, the team and I wanted to showcase a variety of my recipes on the cover in a way that made your mouth water. Hence, this incredible combination of different recipes from within the book has become what is now known as 'the cover-worthy wellness bowl'. It encapsulates everything I love about the food in this book – it's fresh, easy, flavoursome, textural and delicious!

SERVES 6

3 large handfuls of mixed lettuce leaves
2 Lebanese cucumbers, finely sliced
6 radishes, finely sliced
24 cherry tomatoes, halved
½ cup pink sauerkraut
1½ avocados, quartered
1 x quantity 'KFJ' (Kentucky Fried Jackfruit) (see page 147)

VEGAN MAYO (MAKES 560 G)
3 tablespoons extra-virgin olive or macadamia oil
3 tablespoons avocado or hemp seed oil
125 ml (½ cup) coconut oil, chilled
2 teaspoons dijon mustard
½ teaspoon sea salt
2 tablespoons apple cider vinegar
juice of ½ lemon
1 tablespoon maple syrup or coconut nectar

DRESSING
3 tablespoons coconut aminos
1 garlic clove, finely grated
1 cm piece of ginger, peeled and finely grated
zest and juice of 1 lemon
2 tablespoons extra-virgin olive, avocado, macadamia or hemp oil
1 tablespoon apple cider vinegar

TO SERVE
toasted sesame seeds
hemp seeds
chilli flakes
micro herbs
lime wedges

To make the mayo, in a high-speed blender or using a hand-held blender, blitz together the oils, mustard, salt and vinegar and blend until smooth, then add the lemon juice and sweetener and blitz again until completely combined. Transfer to a glass jar with a lid and place in the fridge until needed.

Arrange the lettuce leaves so that they cover the base and side of each serving bowl. Add the cucumber, radish, tomato, sauerkraut, avocado and Kentucky fried jackfruit.

For the dressing, place all the ingredients in a bowl and whisk well to combine.

Drizzle the dressing over the salad and add a generous dollop of vegan mayo. Sprinkle over some sesame seeds, hemp seeds, chilli flakes and micro herbs, add a lime wedge for squeezing and dig in! Leftover mayo will keep in an airtight container in the fridge for up to 1 week, and can be used anywhere you would use regular mayo.

HEALTH TIP *I've included avocado oil in this mayonnaise as it enhances the absorption of important nutrients such as the antioxidant carotenoid found in red cabbage (and in many other fruits and veg). Because fruits and vegetables rich in carotenoids are typically low in fat, we can often miss out on many of the benefits. But not here!*

GREEN TABBOULEH *with* AVOCADO-TAHINI DRESSING

Tabbouleh is, traditionally, a simple Middle Eastern salad of very finely chopped vegetables with lots of parsley and bulgur wheat. My version swaps out the bulgur for nutrient-dense broccoli, adds cucumber and apple to bring a burst of freshness to each and every mouthful and rounds the whole thing off with a creamy green avocado and tahini dressing. What's not to love?

SERVES 4

2 heads of broccoli, stalks discarded, florets roughly chopped
2 tablespoons extra-virgin olive or avocado oil
1 garlic clove, crushed
1 teaspoon sea salt
½ teaspoon freshly ground black pepper
2 Lebanese cucumbers, halved lengthways and finely sliced
2 green apples, cored and sliced
1 long red chilli, finely sliced
2 spring onions, finely sliced
1 handful of mint leaves
1 handful of coriander leaves

AVOCADO-TAHINI DRESSING
1 avocado, smashed
3 tablespoons hulled tahini
1 garlic clove, very finely chopped
3 tablespoons extra-virgin olive, avocado, macadamia or hemp oil
1 tablespoon apple cider vinegar
zest and juice of 1 lemon
sea salt and freshly ground black pepper

Preheat the oven to 180°C and line a baking tray with baking paper.

Add the broccoli, oil, garlic, salt and pepper to a food processor and pulse briefly until the mixture resembles chunky rice.

Spoon the broccoli mixture onto the prepared baking tray and bake for 10–15 minutes, or until some bits begin to brown and char on the edges. Remove from the oven and leave to cool (you can speed up this process by placing it in the fridge).

While the broccoli mixture is cooling, make the dressing. In a small bowl, combine all the ingredients. (The mixture will be quite thick and creamy, so add 1–2 tablespoons of water to loosen it up to your liking if need be.) Season with salt and pepper to taste.

Transfer the roasted broccoli mixture to a large shallow bowl and add the cucumber, apple, chilli, spring onion, half the herbs and half the dressing. Toss well to combine, then drizzle over the remaining dressing. Season well with salt and pepper, scatter over the remaining herbs and serve.

SHAVED FENNEL *with* ORANGE, OLIVES *and* WALNUTS

This salad is one of the easiest recipes in the book, but don't be mistaken, the flavour is up there with some of my all-time favourite creations. If you can't source a blood orange, just swap it out for a regular one or use a ruby grapefruit. Any leftover dressing will keep, refrigerated, for up to 2 weeks.

SERVES 4

2 oranges, peeled and flesh cut into segments
1 blood orange, peeled and flesh cut into segments
2 fennel bulbs, trimmed and very finely shaved, fronds reserved
70 g (½ cup) pitted black olives, sliced
1 large handful of flat-leaf parsley leaves, roughly torn
50 g (½ cup) walnuts, toasted and roughly chopped, plus extra to serve
sea salt and freshly ground black pepper

DRESSING

3 tablespoons extra-virgin olive, avocado, macadamia or hemp oil
1 tablespoon apple cider vinegar
juice of ½ lemon
1 garlic clove, finely grated

Place the dressing ingredients in a jar, screw the lid on and shake well to combine.

Arrange the salad ingredients on a large platter, drizzle with the dressing and season to taste. Top with the reserved fennel fronds and a few extra chopped walnuts and serve.

HEALTH TIP *Apart from being rich in vitamin C, blood oranges also offer unique health benefits associated with high levels of anthocyanins – the red flavonoid pigments that give the blood oranges their intense colour along with their antioxidant properties.*

SPICY SHAVED ASPARAGUS SALAD

It may look fancy but you won't need any special equipment to whip up this delicious salad – the humble vegetable peeler is responsible for the cool ribbon effect you get with the asparagus. If you're not a big fan of chilli, just add less or even leave it out completely, but I think it's a wonderful way to cut through the sharpness of the dressing and the freshness of the pear.

SERVES 4

2 large bunches of asparagus (about 400 g, a mix of colours if possible), woody ends trimmed

2 pears, cored, quartered and finely sliced

2 large handfuls of baby rocket leaves

50 g (½ cup) pecans, toasted and roughly chopped

sea salt and freshly ground black pepper

DRESSING

3 tablespoons extra-virgin olive, avocado, macadamia or hemp oil

2 teaspoons wholegrain mustard

zest and juice of 1 lemon

1 teaspoon chilli flakes

Using a vegetable peeler, shave the asparagus spears lengthways into long ribbons. Place the asparagus ribbons in a large bowl with the pear slices and baby rocket leaves. Set aside.

To make the dressing, add all the ingredients to a bowl or jar and either whisk or shake well.

When ready to serve, pour the dressing over the salad and toss gently to combine, then pile the salad onto a large platter or divide among individual bowls. Sprinkle over the pecans and season with salt and pepper. Enjoy.

HEALTH TIP *Antioxidants are compounds that help protect our cells from the harmful effects of free radicals and oxidative stress. Oxidative stress contributes to ageing, chronic inflammation and many diseases, including cancer. The good news is asparagus, like other green vegetables, is high in antioxidants. These include vitamin E, vitamin C and glutathione, as well as various flavonoids and polyphenols. Time to reach for those spears, I reckon.*

RIBBONED ZUCCHINI SALAD *with*
BABA GANOUSH *and* GARLIC FLATBREADS

*This is one of the most delicious combinations of ingredients. The crispy flatbreads topped
with the creamy baba ganoush and the zucchini is divine. Great for entertaining or just for
a nourishing mid-week meal that feels comforting from the inside out.*

SERVES 4

2 yellow zucchini (or a mix of
  green and yellow)
2 tablespoons extra-virgin olive
  or avocado oil
zest and juice of 1 lemon
sea salt and freshly ground
  black pepper

BABA GANOUSH

1 eggplant, cut into 5 mm thick
  discs
2 pinches of sea salt
1 tablespoon extra-virgin olive or
  avocado oil
zest and juice of 1 lemon
1 large garlic clove, finely grated
2 tablespoons hulled tahini
2 tablespoons coriander leaves
freshly ground black pepper

GARLIC FLATBREADS

100 g (1 cup) almond meal
125 g (1 cup) arrowroot or
  tapioca flour
1 teaspoon garlic powder
125 ml (½ cup) coconut milk
125 ml (½ cup) filtered water, plus
  extra if needed
1 teaspoon sea salt
3–4 tablespoons coconut oil

Using a spiraliser, mandoline, vegetable peeler or sharp knife, cut the
zucchini into long thin ribbons. Place the zucchini ribbons in a bowl
with the oil and lemon zest and juice, and season well with salt and
pepper. Toss together to coat and set aside (the ribbons will soften
nicely as you get on with making the baba ganoush and flatbreads).

For the baba ganoush, set your oven grill to medium heat, position
the rack at the top of the oven and prepare a baking tray with
baking paper. Sprinkle the eggplant discs with a pinch of salt and
place in a colander in the sink to drain any excess liquid. After about
10 minutes, rinse with cold water and pat dry between two thick
paper towels. Arrange the eggplant discs on the baking tray, drizzle
with the oil and sprinkle over another pinch of salt, then grill for
about 10 minutes, turning once or twice, until the eggplant is softened
and golden brown all over. Remove from the tray and, once cool
enough to touch, carefully peel off and discard as much of the skin as
you can. Place the flesh in a food processor, add the lemon zest and
juice, garlic and tahini and mix until smooth and creamy, then add the
coriander and pulse briefly just to incorporate. Season with salt and
pepper to taste and set aside.

To make the flatbreads, combine the almond meal, arrowroot or
tapioca flour, garlic powder, coconut milk, water and salt in a bowl and
mix well to form a smooth, thinnish batter. (The more watery the
batter, the thinner and crispier your flatbreads will be, so add a splash
or two more if you like.)

Melt 1 tablespoon of the coconut oil in a small non-stick frying
pan over medium heat. Add 125 ml (½ cup) of batter to the pan,
tilting and swirling it to coat the base in an even layer, and cook for
2–3 minutes, then carefully turn the flatbread over with a spatula and
cook for a further 2 minutes, or until golden and cooked through.
Lift the flatbread from the pan and set aside wrapped in a clean tea
towel to keep warm. Repeat with the remaining mixture, greasing the
pan with a little coconut oil in between flatbreads to make sure they
don't stick to the pan.

To serve, divide the baba ganoush among plates, top with the zucchini
ribbons and use the flatbreads to scoop up all the deliciousness. Yum.

MUSHROOM CARPACCIO
with PLANT PARMESAN

Raw mushrooms. We've all seen them sitting alone at the salad bar. Sad, dry, untouched. The fact that most recipes call for us to cook these delicious fungi doesn't help their undeservedly bad rap. I tell you what, though, when properly prepared, raw mushrooms can take on delicious flavours that combine with their delightfully soft texture to transform them from zero to salad hero.

SERVES 4

4 large button mushrooms

4 baby portobello (cremini) mushrooms

1 large handful of flat-leaf parsley leaves, finely chopped, plus extra to serve

zest and juice of 1 lemon

2 garlic cloves, very finely chopped

¼ teaspoon sea salt

¼ teaspoon freshly ground black pepper

3 tablespoons extra-virgin olive, avocado, macadamia or hemp oil

2 tablespoons Plant Parmesan (see page 51)

Gently wash the mushrooms and pat them dry on paper towel. Trim off any hard bottom ends, leaving the stalks intact, then cut the mushrooms into thin slices and arrange on a platter so that they overlap slightly.

In a bowl, whisk together the parsley, lemon zest and juice, garlic, salt, pepper and oil to make a dressing.

To serve, drizzle the dressing evenly over the mushrooms and sprinkle over the plant parmesan and a little extra parsley. Enjoy straight away, or leave for 15 minutes, to allow the mushrooms to soften slightly and absorb all the beautiful goodness from the dressing, before eating.

TIP *Confused about the different types of mushroom you see in the store? Both cremini and portobello mushrooms sport a dark brown colour, a smooth cap and have a deep, savoury flavour. Indeed, the only difference between the two seems to be diameter and that's because … they are the same thing! Portobello mushrooms are just the mature version of cremini mushrooms, harvested when they're fully grown.*

Tomato, Fig, Beetroot and Basil

What a combination this plate is. You've got the cooling freshness of sliced tomatoes, the sweetness of velvety figs, the earthiness of sliced baby beetroot and a burst of basil to break the whole thing up. Stripped right back, it lets the ingredients speak for themselves. Using store-bought precooked beetroot here is a very convenient way of making things quick and easy.

SERVES 4

6 precooked baby beetroot, finely sliced
600 g heirloom tomatoes (yellow if possible), finely sliced
6 figs, finely sliced
1 handful of baby basil leaves
sea salt and freshly ground black pepper

DRESSING

2 tablespoons extra-virgin olive, avocado, macadamia or hemp oil
2 tablespoons balsamic vinegar or coconut aminos
juice of 1 lemon

Spread your beetroot, tomato and fig slices over a large platter in a messy, overlapping manner. Scatter over the baby basil leaves.

In a small bowl, whisk together the dressing ingredients.

Drizzle the dressing over the salad, season with salt and pepper and enjoy.

HEALTH TIP *Calcium is vital for strong bones and figs are a great plant-based source, so get them into you as part of this delicious salad.*

GRILLED PEACH *with* FENNEL *and* RADICCHIO

I understand that raw fennel isn't necessarily everyone's cup of tea, but don't rule this salad out if that 'everyone' just happens to be you! Here I have balanced the fennel's aniseedy, liquorice flavour – and the bitterness of the radicchio – with the saltiness of baby capers and the juicy sweetness of grilled peach. Pretty clever, huh?

SERVES 4

4 yellow or white peaches, stones removed, cut into wedges
1 tablespoon extra-virgin olive or avocado oil
2 fennel bulbs, finely shaved, fronds reserved
1 treviso radicchio, leaves separated
1 tablespoon salted baby capers, rinsed

DRESSING
3 tablespoons extra-virgin olive, avocado, macadamia or hemp oil
zest and juice of 1 lemon
1 small handful of chervil or flat-leaf parsley leaves, finely chopped
1 tablespoon apple cider vinegar
sea salt and freshly ground black pepper

Heat a barbecue grill plate to hot or place a chargrill pan over high heat.

Coat the peach wedges in the oil, then cook for 1–2 minutes on each side, or until slightly softened and beautifully charred. Set aside on a plate.

In a large bowl, toss together the shaved fennel, radicchio leaves and capers.

To make the dressing, add all the ingredients to a bowl or jar and either whisk or shake well. Season to taste with salt and pepper.

Add the peaches to the salad, pour over the dressing and toss gently to ensure everything is well coated. To serve, pile the salad onto a serving platter or divide among bowls and scatter over the reserved fennel fronds. Enjoy.

HEALTH TIP *Treviso radicchio is a member of the chicory family with a mild flavour, a shape like a baby cos lettuce, and long purple leaves and thick white ribs. Its slightly bitter leaves have a firm texture and are high in potassium, magnesium and vitamin C.*

RAW ZUCCHINI SALAD *with* OLIVES *and* PINE NUTS

Whenever I make this dish I think about the first time I enjoyed it ... it was a warm summer's day, I was sitting outside enjoying a refreshing breeze and, while I was slowly savouring each mouthful, I actually caught myself saying 'yum' out loud. I hope it gives you a 'yum' moment, too.

SERVES 4

2 green or yellow zucchini
generous pinch of sea salt
3 tablespoons pitted olives
   (kalamata work well), drained
   and quartered
2 tablespoons pine nuts, toasted
1 teaspoon chilli flakes
2 tablespoons roughly chopped
   mint or flat-leaf parsley leaves
freshly ground black pepper

DRESSING
juice of 1 lemon
2 tablespoons extra-virgin olive,
   avocado, macadamia or hemp oil
1 tablespoon apple cider vinegar
1 garlic clove, very finely chopped

Using a spiraliser, mandoline or sharp knife, cut the zucchini into long thin ribbons, then transfer to a colander and season with the salt. Set aside for 3–4 minutes to let the salt draw out some moisture.

Meanwhile, to make the dressing, whisk together all the ingredients in a small bowl.

Pat dry the zucchini ribbons with paper towel, then arrange them on a large platter. Drizzle over the dressing and leave to chill in the fridge for 20 minutes, or until the acid in the dressing has done its job and softened the zucchini nicely. Scatter over the olives, pine nuts, chilli and chopped herbs, season well with salt and pepper and enjoy.

AMAZING AVOCADO SALAD
with MACADAMIA PESTO

The truth is, not everyone loves coriander. Interestingly enough, it doesn't just come down to personal preference, it's all about our genetic make-up – some people are just predisposed to finding the taste really yuck. Although it makes an appearance in lots of my sauces, dressings and pestos (such as the one below) be aware that you can always sub it out for mint or extra flat-leaf parsley if need be. However you like to roll when it comes to herbs, I recommend you make up a double batch of this pesto and try it out with some of my other recipes – you won't regret it.

SERVES 4

2 avocados, halved
1 Lebanese cucumber, halved lengthways and finely sliced diagonally
2 radishes, finely sliced
120 g (2 cups) alfalfa sprouts
3 tablespoons extra-virgin olive oil
3 tablespoons macadamia nuts, toasted
sea salt and freshly ground black pepper

MACADAMIA PESTO (MAKES 250 G)
1 bunch of flat-leaf parsley, leaves and stalks roughly chopped
1 bunch of coriander or mint, leaves picked
125 ml (½ cup) extra-virgin olive, avocado, macadamia or hemp oil
3 tablespoons macadamia nuts
zest and juice of 1 lemon
1 tablespoon apple cider vinegar
1 teaspoon chilli flakes
generous pinch of sea salt

For the pesto, place all the ingredients in a food processor or high-speed blender and blitz until well combined.

To serve, place a spoonful or two of the pesto in the centre of each serving plate and spread it out a little with the back of the spoon. (Any leftover pesto will keep in an airtight container in the fridge for up to 1 week and makes a great dip for roasted veg or a topping for pizzas.)

Finely slice the avocado halves and arrange them evenly over the pesto. Top with the cucumber, radish and alfalfa sprouts, drizzle over the extra-virgin olive oil and scatter over the macadamia nuts to finish. Season well with salt and pepper and enjoy.

HEALTH TIP *Alfalfa sprouts are the shoots of the alfalfa plant, harvested before they become the full-grown plant. Because they are so small, the sprouts contain a concentrated amount of vitamins and minerals such as calcium, vitamin K and vitamin C.*

SOUPY, Saucy — and — SAUTEED

SPICY PUMPKIN SOUP *with* MACADAMIA CREAM *and* PUMPKIN CHIPS

I am all about using the entire vegetable when I can, which is why this recipe is a favourite of mine. For this soup, rather than discarding the pumpkin skin, it is roasted until golden brown, crispy and delicious. You won't be needing a bread roll when you've got these crispy pumpkin chips for dipping.

SERVES 4

3 tablespoons melted coconut oil
1 onion, finely diced
2 long red chillies, finely diced
2 garlic cloves, finely diced
½ teaspoon ground coriander
½ teaspoon ground cumin
1 tablespoon red curry paste
  (optional, see Tip)
1 kg butternut pumpkin, cut into
  small chunks, skin reserved
  and cut into rough pieces
1 large sweet potato, peeled and
  roughly chopped
1 litre (4 cups) vegetable stock
  (see page 88 for homemade)
  or filtered water
sea salt and freshly ground
  black pepper
2 teaspoons chilli flakes
80 ml (⅓ cup) extra-virgin
  olive oil

MACADAMIA CREAM
(MAKES 200 G)
160 g (1 cup) macadamias,
  soaked in warm water for
  1 hour or overnight, drained
125 ml (½ cup) coconut milk or
  coconut cream, plus extra to
  get it to the consistency of
  pouring cream
juice of ½ lemon
½ teaspoon sea salt

Preheat the oven to 220°C and line a baking tray with baking paper.

For the macadamia cream, blitz together all the ingredients in a food processor until smooth and creamy. Set aside.

Heat 2 tablespoons of the coconut oil in a large, heavy-based saucepan over medium–high heat. Add the onion and chilli and saute for 2–3 minutes, or until softened. Add the garlic, coriander, cumin and curry paste, if using, and saute for a further 2–3 minutes, or until the garlic has softened and caramelised and the curry paste is aromatic.

Add the pumpkin and sweet potato to the pan, pour over the stock or water and bring to the boil, then reduce the heat to a simmer and cook, uncovered, for 30 minutes, or until your vegetables are soft enough to mash with a fork.

Meanwhile, coat the pumpkin skin pieces in the remaining coconut oil and transfer to the prepared baking tray. Season well with salt and pepper and roast for 15–20 minutes, or until golden brown and crispy around the edges.

Remove the saucepan from the heat and, using a hand-held blender, blitz your soup ingredients together to a smooth puree. Season with salt and pepper to taste, then return to the heat and warm through.

To serve, divide the soup among bowls and swirl a tablespoon of the macadamia cream into each. Sprinkle over the chilli flakes, drizzle over the olive oil and top with the crispy pumpkin shards.

TIP I recommend using a red curry paste here, so if you don't make your own, be sure to keep an eye out for added seed oils and refined sugars in any store-bought option. The ingredients should be simple and celebrate real food without any unnecessary additives and fillers.

Simple Mushroom Soup

The awesome thing about using mushrooms for a soup is that they cook relatively quickly compared to other vegetables. Sauteing them first like this releases all their lovely mushroomy flavours, giving this dish loads of depth and warmth.

SERVES 4

2 tablespoons coconut oil
1 onion, chopped
4 garlic cloves, finely chopped
800 g mushrooms (button, swiss brown or a mix of varieties), sliced
500 ml (2 cups) vegetable stock (see page 88 for homemade)
500 ml (2 cups) coconut milk
1 teaspoon dried thyme
1 teaspoon oregano leaves
sea salt and freshly ground black pepper
2 tablespoons finely chopped flat-leaf parsley leaves

Melt the coconut oil in a large, heavy-based saucepan over medium–high heat, add the onion and garlic and saute until translucent. Add the mushrooms and saute until they have softened, reduced in size slightly and started to brown, about 5–6 minutes.

Pour the vegetable stock and coconut milk into the pan, stir in the thyme and oregano and season well with salt and pepper to taste. Bring to the boil, then reduce the heat to low and simmer for 5–6 minutes, or until slightly thickened.

Ladle the soup into bowls, sprinkle over the parsley and enjoy.

TIP *This is a perfect whip-it-together meal for having on the table in 15 minutes. If you prefer a thicker, creamier soup, add the mushrooms whole, simmer for slightly longer, then blitz with a hand-held blender to reduce it to a really lovely cream of mushroom soup. Winning.*

ROASTED COCONUT *and* CAULIFLOWER SOUP

This soup has got to be one of the easiest to make. It doesn't need much attention and is lovely and rich, lightly spiced and deliciously creamy. Perfect served steaming hot in winter or as a cold soup in the peak of summer.

SERVES 4

1 head of cauliflower (about 800 g), cut into even-sized florets
2 onions, roughly diced
4 garlic cloves, unpeeled
1 teaspoon ground cinnamon
1 teaspoon ground coriander
2 tablespoons melted coconut oil
55 g (1 cup) coconut flakes
400 ml can coconut milk
600 ml vegetable stock (see page 88 for homemade) or filtered water, plus extra if needed
sea salt and freshly ground black pepper
3 tablespoons extra-virgin olive or avocado oil

Preheat the oven to 180°C and line two baking trays with baking paper.

Place the cauliflower, onion and garlic on one of the prepared trays, sprinkle over the spices, drizzle over the coconut oil and toss everything together. Roast for 25–30 minutes, or until the vegetables are cooked through and a little charred on the edges.

When the vegetables are almost done, scatter the coconut flakes over the other tray and roast for 3–4 minutes, or until golden brown, then remove from the oven and set aside to cool.

Once the vegetables are ready, set aside the garlic cloves and ½ cup of the cauliflower and scrape the rest of the vegetables into a large saucepan set over medium heat. Squeeze the garlic cloves out of their skins and add them to the pan together with the coconut milk and vegetable stock or water. Bring to the boil, then reduce the heat to a simmer and cook for 5 minutes, uncovered, until reduced. Remove from the heat and, using a hand-held blender, blitz the soup until smooth and creamy, adding a splash more stock or water if it is too thick for your liking.

Season well with salt and pepper, drizzle over the oil and serve topped with the reserved cauliflower and the coconut flakes.

HEALTH TIP *Well, you know I love cauliflower in all its forms, but did you know that along with being a great lower carb alternative to grains, breads and rice in some recipes, it also contains 77 per cent of your daily intake of vitamin C? Move over oranges!*

Spicy Peanut Stew

I first tried a dish similar to this about 10 years ago when I was backpacking around the coastal region of Sihanoukville in Cambodia. The region is renowned for spicy vegetable curries and soups and this one truly blew me away, so I thought it only fitting I create an updated take on it.

SERVES 4

2 tablespoons coconut oil

4 garlic cloves, very finely chopped

5 cm piece of ginger, peeled and finely chopped

1 red onion, roughly chopped

1 long red chilli, roughly chopped

1 teaspoon sea salt

1.5 litres (6 cups) vegetable stock (see page 88 for homemade)

250 g (1 cup) unsalted peanut butter (I like chunky)

125 g (½ cup) tomato paste

1 bunch of kale (about 300 g), stalks discarded, leaves chopped into 2.5 cm strips

2 teaspoons chilli flakes, or to taste

TO SERVE

800 g (4 cups) Cauliflower Rice (see page 125)

3 tablespoons chopped roasted peanuts

Melt the coconut oil in a large, heavy-based saucepan over medium–high heat, add the garlic, ginger, onion, chilli and salt and saute for 4–5 minutes, or until the garlic and onion are softened, caramelised and fragrant. Pour in the vegetable stock and bring to the boil, then lower the heat to medium–low and simmer for 10–15 minutes, or until reduced by about a third.

Combine the peanut butter and tomato paste in a large heatproof bowl. Transfer 500 ml (2 cups) of the hot stock to the bowl and whisk to combine, then pour the mixture back into the soup and mix well. Stir in the kale and chilli flakes, return to a simmer and cook for a further 15 minutes, stirring often, until the stew has thickened and the greens have softened.

Serve the stew on a bed of cauliflower rice and top with a sprinkling of chopped peanuts.

TIP *I recommend trying this stew as it is first, but if you want to bulk it out a little, you can always add sweet potato. Simply toss in a chopped sweet potato when you bring the stock to the boil.*

JACKFRUIT CURRY

Jackfruit is a healthy alternative to meat in savoury dishes like this delicious curry, where it is simmered in coconut milk, ginger, chilli and spices. Jackfruit is now becoming more readily available at major supermarkets, but if your local doesn't stock it yet, you'll be able to pick it up easily at your local health food store. It is most commonly found canned, just make sure the one you buy comes in brine and is not flavoured with sauces or syrups.

SERVES 4

1 tablespoon coconut oil
1 onion, diced
1 kg canned young jackfruit in water, drained and rinsed
400 ml can coconut milk
125 ml (½ cup) vegetable stock (see page 88 for homemade)
2 fresh or dried bay leaves
zest and juice of 1 lime
80 g (½ cup) roasted peanuts, roughly chopped
1 handful of Thai basil leaves
1 small handful of coriander leaves
800 g (4 cups) Cauliflower Rice (see page 125) (optional)

CURRY PASTE
5 cm piece of ginger, peeled
2 garlic cloves, very finely chopped
2 teaspoons ground turmeric
1 bird's eye chilli or ½ teaspoon chilli flakes
1 teaspoon mustard seeds
1 teaspoon fennel seeds
1 teaspoon fenugreek seeds (optional)
½ teaspoon sea salt

To make the curry paste, pound all the ingredients together with a pestle and mortar or pulse together briefly in a food processor to form a paste.

Melt the coconut oil in a large saucepan over medium–high heat. Add the onion and cook for 3 minutes, or until softened and caramelised, then stir in the prepared spice paste and cook, stirring, for 2–3 minutes, or until fragrant.

Meanwhile, using a sharp knife, cut off and discard any parts of the jackfruit that are hard or contain seeds.

Pour the coconut milk and vegetable stock into the pan and stir in the jackfruit and bay leaves. Bring to the boil, then reduce the heat to a simmer and leave to cook, uncovered and stirring occasionally, for 30 minutes, or until the curry has reduced. Stir in the lime zest and juice and half the peanuts, then remove from the heat. Taste and add a little salt if necessary.

To serve, divide the curry among plates and scatter over the basil, coriander and the remaining peanuts. Enjoy with cauliflower rice, if you like.

TIP *Jackfruit is a species of tree in the fig, mulberry and breadfruit family. The huge trees produce massive, green, oblong fruits with a bumpy, fleshy exterior. On the inside, jackfruit contains many pale-yellow, plump bulbs, which are edible and joined at the core. The seeds can also be cooked, eaten on their own, or ground into flour. When it's unripe, the jackfruit has more of a neutral flavour, like a potato, and works well in savoury dishes like this; when eaten ripe and raw, the taste of jackfruit is sweet and similar to pineapple, mango and banana.*

SAUTEED ASPARAGUS
with ROMESCO

I don't know about you, but I often think that pan-fried veggies need a sauce. At a pinch, you might use hummus, extra-virgin olive oil, coconut aminos, or whatever else you have hanging out in your fridge or pantry. But if you have some extra time up your sleeve, I suggest you show your food processor some love and whip up this romesco sauce. You won't regret it.

SERVES 4

2 tablespoons extra-virgin olive or avocado oil
2 large bunches of asparagus (about 400 g), woody ends trimmed
sea salt and freshly ground black pepper

ROMESCO SAUCE
1 red capsicum, halved and deseeded
1 tablespoon tomato paste
1 garlic clove
½ teaspoon smoked paprika
¼ teaspoon cayenne pepper
2 tablespoons apple cider vinegar
3 tablespoons toasted almonds, plus 1 tablespoon extra, roughly chopped, to serve

Preheat the oven to 200°C and line a baking tray with baking paper.

For the romesco sauce, place the capsicum on the prepared tray, transfer to the oven and roast, turning occasionally, until the skin is charred and blistered. Transfer the capsicum to an airtight container, tightly seal with the lid and set aside for 10 or so minutes to steam (the steam helps to lift the skin). When ready, peel off the capsicum skin and discard, being sure not to rinse the flesh as this can spoil the flavour. Transfer the capsicum to a food processor or blender together with the remaining sauce ingredients and blitz to a chunky paste. Set aside.

Warm the oil in a large frying pan or chargrill pan over medium heat. Add the asparagus, in batches if necessary, and saute, tossing regularly, for 4–5 minutes, or until the asparagus softens slightly and starts to char.

Remove the asparagus from the pan and pile onto a serving platter. Spoon over the romesco, sprinkle with the extra chopped almonds and enjoy.

TIP *When it comes to marinades, pestos and sauces like this romesco, I always like to double the recipe so that I have extra on hand for other delicious recipes later in the week. Try it yourself and you'll soon find you have heaps of options in your fridge to help keep your healthy eating on track.*

CRISPY FRIED MIXED GREENS *with* BLACK OLIVE DRESSING

This recipe is a great example of how you can take a nice variety of delicious greens, throw them together quickly in a pan, and then really bring them to life with an awesome dressing. It makes a perfect dinner or platter to share. Feel free to experiment with the greens in this recipe – I love the ones listed below, but you can use whatever you have in your fridge.

SERVES 4

2 tablespoons coconut oil

1 bunch of broccolini (about 200 g)

12 brussels sprouts, quartered

1 large bunch of rainbow chard (about 400 g), leaves roughly torn and stalks roughly chopped (see Tip)

1 leek, white part only, finely sliced

zest and juice of 1 lemon

sea salt and freshly ground black pepper

BLACK OLIVE DRESSING

135 g (1 cup) pitted black olives, roughly chopped

1 bird's eye chilli, deseeded and roughly chopped

1 garlic clove, very finely chopped

3 tablespoons extra-virgin olive, avocado, macadamia or hemp oil

1 tablespoon finely chopped flat-leaf parsley leaves

1 tablespoon finely chopped coriander leaves

sea salt and freshly ground black pepper

For the black olive dressing, add the olives, chilli, garlic and oil to a bowl and mix well to combine. Gently stir in the herbs and season well with salt and pepper. Set aside.

Melt the coconut oil in a large frying pan over medium–high heat. Add the broccolini, brussels sprouts and rainbow chard stalks and saute for 5–6 minutes, or until they begin to soften and turn golden brown at the edges. Add the leek and rainbow chard leaves and continue to cook, stirring, for 5–6 minutes, or until the chard leaves have softened and the leek has begun to caramelise.

Divide the greens among plates or pile onto a large platter and top with a generous helping of the black olive dressing (any leftovers will keep in an airtight container in the fridge for up to 2 weeks). Squeeze over the lemon juice, sprinkle over the lemon zest and season well with salt and pepper. Enjoy.

TIP *Rainbow chard has varying tastes depending on which part you eat. The large, firm leaves are sweet, earthy and just slightly bitter, like a milder spinach. The stalks, which can be white, yellow, red, purple, pink or striped, resemble celery and have a sweet taste that is reminiscent of beetroot.*

GARLICKY SAUTEED GREENS

In contrast to this recipe's crispier cousin (see page 86), this is all about soft, tender and beautifully sauteed veg. The stock or water really helps transform the usually quite dense leaves into something that is both easy to digest and singing with flavour. Again, like with most of my 'green' recipes, you can mix and match the veg varieties here to make it work for you and your tastebuds (and what you have in the house).

I've given details here for a delicious vegetable stock. It is easy to make, but if you choose to purchase one, make sure it doesn't contain any nasties and sticks to the basics of filtered water, vegetables, herbs and spices.

SERVES 4

2 tablespoons coconut oil
½ bunch of rainbow chard
  (about 400 g), leaves and stalks
  separated and roughly chopped
4 garlic cloves, very finely chopped
250 ml (1 cup) vegetable stock
  (see below) or filtered water
1 bunch of kale (about 300 g),
  stalks discarded and leaves
  roughly chopped
½ bunch of English spinach (about
  100 g), stalks discarded and
  leaves roughly chopped
zest and juice of 1 lemon, plus
  lemon wedges to serve
2 tablespoons Plant Parmesan (see
  page 51) (optional)
sea salt and freshly ground
  black pepper

BASIC VEGETABLE STOCK

1 tablespoon coconut, extra-virgin
  olive or avocado oil
1 onion, skin on, roughly chopped
4 garlic cloves, unpeeled, roughly
  chopped
4 carrots, unpeeled, roughly
  chopped
4 celery stalks, roughly chopped
sea salt and freshly ground
  black pepper
2 litres (8 cups) filtered water
1 large handful of your favourite
  chopped soft herbs (parsley,
  coriander and basil all work
  well here)
4 rosemary sprigs
2 fresh or dried bay leaves

To make the stock, heat the oil in a large, heavy-based saucepan over medium–high heat. Add the onion, garlic, carrot and celery and season well with salt and pepper. Saute for 2–3 minutes, or until the veg are slightly softened, aromatic and caramelised around the edges. Pour over the water, add the chopped herbs, rosemary and bay leaves and bring to the boil, then reduce the heat to low, cover with a lid and simmer for 45–60 minutes. Leave to cool slightly before straining into a suitable airtight container. The stock will keep refrigerated for up to 2 weeks or frozen for up to 3 months.

Melt the oil in a large frying pan over medium–high heat, add the chard stalks and garlic and saute for 2–3 minutes, or until softened, lightly golden and fragrant.

Add the stock to the pan and bring to the boil, then reduce the heat to a simmer. Add the chard leaves and cook for 2–3 minutes, or until just softened. Add the kale and cook for another 2–3 minutes before adding the spinach and cooking for a final 2–3 minutes (the greens cook at different rates, hence putting them in at different times – they will be lovely, soft and silky when they're ready). Squeeze over the lemon juice and stir in the lemon zest, then divide among plates or pile onto a platter.

Scatter over the plant parmesan (if using), season well with salt and pepper and serve with the lemon wedges for squeezing. You're good to go!

CURRIED CAULIFLOWER STEAKS
with MINTY RAITA

My crispy cauliflower steaks were such a hit in my previous book, Smart Carbs, that I just had to show you what I have been doing with them since. I think curry powder and cauliflower is a match made in heaven, and even more so when that lovely spiced, charred cauli is paired with a cooling minty raita. Try it and I guarantee you'll be cooking this more than once a week.

SERVES 4

2 large heads of cauliflower
2 tablespoons coconut, extra-virgin
  olive or avocado oil
1 tablespoon curry powder
2 teaspoons chilli flakes
½ teaspoon ground turmeric
sea salt and freshly ground
  black pepper
juice of 1 lemon
fried curry leaves, to serve
  (optional; see Tip)

MINTY RAITA
350 g (1½ cups) coconut yoghurt
1 Lebanese cucumber, deseeded
  and diced
2 large handfuls of mint leaves,
  finely chopped
1 teaspoon chopped dill fronds
½ teaspoon smoked paprika
½ teaspoon ground cumin
zest and juice of 1 lemon
sea salt and freshly ground black
  pepper, to taste

To make the raita, scoop the coconut yoghurt into a bowl. Add the remaining ingredients and stir well to combine, adding a little of the clear coconut liquid from the yoghurt tub to loosen it if necessary (you can keep the rest for smoothies). The raita should be thick and chunky. Transfer to the fridge to chill for at least 1 hour (it will keep in an airtight container in the fridge for up to 1 week).

Preheat the oven to 180°C and line a baking tray with baking paper.

Sit the cauliflowers upright on your chopping board and cut four even slices about 2 cm thick out of each, to make eight slices in total.

Heat the oil in a frying pan over high heat. Add one of the cauliflower steaks and fry for 4 minutes, turning halfway through, or until nicely caramelised. Transfer the caramelised steak to the prepared baking tray and repeat with the remaining cauliflower steaks.

Sprinkle the curry powder, chilli flakes and turmeric over the cauliflower steaks to coat evenly and season well with salt and pepper. Roast for 20–30 minutes, or until the cauliflower steaks are cooked through and golden brown at the edges.

To serve, divide your cauliflower steaks among plates and top each with a generous dollop of minty raita, a squeeze of lemon juice and some crispy fried curry leaves, if you like.

TIP *I have used curry leaves here as a topping for a very good reason, not just because they look great! They are popular in Ayurvedic medicine and can help to improve digestion. To crisp them up, simply fry them in a hot pan with a little coconut oil.*

Roasted, BAKED and BARBECUED

CRISPY BRUSSELS SPROUTS
with SRIRACHA CHILLI SAUCE

Ever tried to make crispy brussels sprouts but couldn't get them charred and crunchy enough? Well, I have a few hot tips that will give you the perfect brussels every time. The key to crisping lies in three different areas: temperature, oil and size. Most of the time people either don't cook their sprouts at a high enough temperature or add enough oil (or both). You want them to be well-coated with olive, avocado or coconut oil – this is not the time for a light drizzle. And when it comes to the best sauce for perfectly cooked brussels? Well, I don't think you can go past the heat from this awesome sriracha chilli sauce.

SERVES 4

500 g brussels sprouts, trimmed
and halved lengthways

3 tablespoons coconut, extra-virgin
olive or avocado oil

sea salt and freshly ground
black pepper

**SRIRACHA CHILLI SAUCE
(MAKES 400 G)**

300 g long red chillies

1½ tablespoons extra-virgin
olive oil

3 garlic cloves, crushed

1½ tablespoons apple cider
vinegar

1 tablespoon tomato paste

1 tablespoon coconut aminos

2 teaspoons maple syrup or
coconut nectar

½ teaspoon sea salt

For the sriracha chilli sauce, place all the ingredients in a food processor and blitz until smooth. Transfer the mixture to a saucepan over high heat and bring to the boil, stirring often. Reduce the heat to a simmer and cook for 8–10 minutes, stirring occasionally, until the sauce has thickened and reduced slightly. Remove from the heat and leave to cool completely. (The sriracha will keep in an airtight container in the fridge for up to 2 weeks.)

Preheat the oven to 220°C and line two baking trays with baking paper.

Add the brussels to a large bowl, drizzle over the oil, season well with salt and pepper and mix well. Spread the coated brussels, cut-side down, over the prepared baking trays in a single layer, then transfer to the oven and roast until crispy, browned and tender, about 25–30 minutes.

Remove the brussels from the oven and season with a little salt and pepper to taste. Serve alongside the delicious sriracha chilli sauce.

TIP *Originating in Thailand, sriracha is frequently used as a dipping sauce, particularly for seafood. In neighbouring Vietnam, it is often used as a condiment for pho and fried noodles, and as a topping for spring rolls. These days you can see sriracha everywhere – from eggs and burgers, to jams, cocktails, potato chips and even lollipops. So, once you've made up your batch, you can use the remainder in pretty much any way you like!*

THAI-STYLE ROASTED PUMPKIN WEDGES *with* AVOCADO DRESSING *and* CRUNCHY SEEDS

Picking a favourite recipe is a bit like having to choose a favourite child. I mean ... we all have one, don't we? The truth is, this recipe is my ultimate favourite in this book. I love pumpkin full-stop, I love this zesty avocado dressing and I really love how simple, easy and flavoursome the whole thing is. I hope you like it as much as I do!

SERVES 4

1 kent pumpkin (about 2 kg), unpeeled, deseeded and cut into large wedges
1 tablespoon melted coconut oil
1 teaspoon ground cumin
1 teaspoon ground coriander
sea salt and freshly ground black pepper
2 tablespoons pumpkin seeds, lightly toasted
1 small handful of coriander leaves
1 lime, cut into cheeks, to serve

AVOCADO DRESSING

125 ml (½ cup) extra-virgin olive, avocado, macadamia or hemp oil
1 avocado
1 handful of coriander leaves
1 tablespoon apple cider vinegar
1 teaspoon chilli powder
zest and juice of 1 lime
pinch of sea salt

Preheat the oven to 180°C and line a large baking tray with baking paper.

Place the pumpkin wedges on the prepared tray and, using your hands, massage in the oil and spices to coat well. Season generously with salt and pepper and bake for about 45 minutes, or until the pumpkin is soft and caramelised, with crispy skin and a lovely golden brown colour on the outside.

While your pumpkin is cooking, make the avocado dressing. Add all the ingredients to a food processor and blitz until well combined, smooth and creamy. Set aside.

To serve, divide the pumpkin wedges among plates or pile onto a large platter and drizzle over the avocado dressing. Scatter over the toasted pumpkin seeds and coriander and serve with the lime cheeks for squeezing.

TIP *If you've got the time and are feeling extra creative, try whipping up a batch of Vegan Mayo (see page 52) and serve it up with this. Trust me, it'll deliver the most awesome flavour sensation.*

ROASTED BABY CAULIS
with HARISSA PASTE

Harissa is a fiery red-orange North African paste that has become very popular in the culinary world in recent years, both for its flavour and versatility in the kitchen. I've given you a simplified version of the traditional recipe, made with ingredients that I think most of you will already have in your kitchen. I have also used baby cauliflowers here because they look amazing and cook much more quickly than large cauliflowers, but feel free to use a large one instead – just be sure to extend the cooking time a little.

SERVES 4

125 ml (½ cup) extra-virgin olive oil
4–6 baby cauliflowers, leaves on
   if possible
sea salt and freshly ground
   black pepper
Vegan Mayo (see page 52), to serve
1 handful of coriander leaves,
   to serve

HARISSA PASTE

3 tablespoons tomato paste
2 long red chillies, roughly chopped
3 tablespoons extra-virgin olive,
   avocado, macadamia or hemp oil
2 garlic cloves, crushed
½ teaspoon sea salt
1 teaspoon cumin seeds or ground
   cumin
1 teaspoon coriander seeds or
   ground coriander
1 teaspoon sweet or smoked paprika
zest and juice of 1 lemon
1 handful of coriander leaves

Preheat the oven to 180°C and line a baking tray with baking paper.

To make the harissa paste, blitz all the ingredients in a food processor until smooth.

In a bowl, whisk together the oil and 2–3 tablespoons of the harissa paste. For a thicker, spicier sauce use more harissa, for a lighter, thinner sauce add less. Leftover harissa paste will keep in an airtight container in the fridge for 2–3 weeks.

Place your baby cauliflowers on the prepared baking tray and coat them with the harissa oil, massaging it into all sides with your hands to ensure you get good coverage. Season well with salt and pepper and roast for 45–60 minutes, or until the cauliflowers are cooked through and the outsides are golden brown and crispy.

To serve, place the tray in the middle of the table on a heatproof board or tea towel. Using a sharp knife, slice open the cauliflowers, then dollop over some mayo and sprinkle over the coriander leaves. Tuck in.

HEALTH TIP *Did you know that a chilli's bright colour signals its high levels of vitamin A? Often called the anti-infection vitamin, vitamin A is essential for healthy mucous membranes which line the nasal passages, lungs, intestinal tract and urinary tract, and serve as the body's first line of defence against invading pathogens.*

CHARRED COS *with* CHILLI *and* MACADAMIAS

I first tried charred cos in San Francisco. Whenever I travel I put together a list of healthy restaurants and cafes that I have researched before I get to each location. This type of forward planning is a super handy way to stay on track and eat really well on the road because you're never left wondering where to find something healthy. I was stoked to find this on a menu and I went back for seconds the next day!

SERVES 4

3 tablespoons macadamia nuts
3 tablespoons extra-virgin olive oil
1 tablespoon chilli flakes
sea salt and freshly ground
    black pepper
4 baby cos lettuces, halved
    lengthways
2 lemons, cut into cheeks or
    wedges

Place the macadamia nuts in a frying pan over medium–high heat and dry-fry for 3–4 minutes, tossing frequently, until toasted and golden brown all over. Remove from the heat and smash roughly using a mortar and pestle. Set aside.

Heat a barbecue grill plate to medium or place a chargrill pan over medium heat.

In a bowl, whisk together the oil, chilli flakes and a pinch of salt and pepper.

Brush the cos halves with the olive oil mixture, then transfer, cut-side down, to the barbecue or pan and cook for 2–3 minutes on each side, or until nicely charred all over.

Transfer the charred cos to a large serving dish. Squeeze over a lemon cheek and sprinkle over the toasted smashed macadamias. Season well with salt and pepper and serve with the rest of the lemon cheeks or wedges for squeezing.

HEALTH TIP *For those who follow a low-carb lifestyle, it doesn't get much more low-carb than cos lettuce! With just 1–2 grams of carbohydrate per cup, this should be your go-to green for minerals such as calcium, phosphorous, magnesium and potassium.*

HERBY HASSELBACKS
with SALSA VERDE

*Not to be confused with herby David Hasselhoffs, these herby hasselback sweet potatoes
are really delicious and easy to make, yet quite impressive. Their fanned tops get
beautifully browned and crispy in the oven while the insides remain nice and soft. I like to
baste mine in a garlicky, herby salsa verde to give them lots of extra flavour.*

SERVES 4

4 small sweet potatoes (about
   800 g), unpeeled
3 tablespoons extra-virgin olive oil
1 teaspoon finely chopped fresh
   or dried rosemary
1 teaspoon finely chopped fresh
   or dried thyme
2 garlic cloves, very finely chopped
1 teaspoon chilli flakes
1 teaspoon lemon zest (optional)
sea salt and freshly ground
   black pepper

SALSA VERDE
1 large handful of basil leaves, plus
   extra to serve
1 large handful of flat-leaf parsley,
   stalks and leaves
¼ red onion, finely chopped
2 garlic cloves, very finely chopped
3 tablespoons extra-virgin olive,
   avocado, macadamia or hemp oil
zest and juice of 1 lime

Preheat the oven to 180°C and line a large baking tray with
baking paper.

Using a sharp knife, make deep incisions 2–3 mm across each sweet
potato, ensuring you don't cut right down to the bottom so that they
hold together.

Place the sweet potatoes on the prepared tray, then brush with
1 tablespoon of the olive oil and bake for 30 minutes.

Whisk the rosemary, thyme and garlic in a bowl with the remaining
2 tablespoons of olive oil. Set aside.

To make the salsa verde, add all the ingredients to a food processor
and blitz to form a rough paste.

Remove the sweet potatoes from the oven and spoon the herby
oil over the top. Return to the oven and bake for another 15 minutes,
or until the sweet potatoes are browned on top and cooked all the
way through.

To serve, divide the hasselbacks among plates and sprinkle with
the chilli flakes and lemon zest, if you like. Season with salt and
pepper, drizzle over the salsa verde and scatter over a few basil
leaves to finish.

HEALTH TIP *Ever wondered why sweet potatoes are actually
sweet? Well, when you heat sweet potatoes, an enzyme starts
breaking down their starch into a sugar called maltose. Maltose
isn't as sweet as table sugar and, interestingly, you can control
the sweetness of sweet potatoes somewhat by how you cook them.
Cooking sweet potatoes quickly, for instance, by steaming them or
cutting them into smaller pieces before roasting, can reduce their
ultimate sweetness. On the other hand, cooking sweet potatoes
slowly on low heat will give that maltose-making enzyme more
time to convert the starch into sugar, giving you sweeter sweet
potatoes. Sweet!*

ROASTED RED CABBAGE WEDGES *with* MUSTARD VINAIGRETTE

Turning the humble red cabbage into a delicious meal is as easy as a hot oven and a tangy vinaigrette. The result is a versatile, inexpensive dish that will have you feeling good from the inside out. While cabbage may look a lot like lettuce, it actually belongs to the brassica family of vegetables, which includes broccoli, cauliflower and kale, and we know what nutrient powerhouses they are! So, what are you waiting for? It's time to get eating.

SERVES 4

1 red cabbage, outer leaves
  discarded, cut into **8** wedges
3 tablespoons extra-virgin olive oil
sea salt and freshly ground
  black pepper

MUSTARD VINAIGRETTE

3 tablespoons extra-virgin olive,
  avocado, macadamia or hemp oil
1 tablespoon dijon mustard
1 tablespoon wholegrain mustard
1 tablespoon maple syrup or
  coconut nectar
1 tablespoon apple cider vinegar
1 teaspoon coconut aminos
  (optional)

Preheat the oven to 220°C and line a baking tray with baking paper.

Lay the cabbage wedges, cut-side down, on the prepared tray, drizzle over the oil and season well with salt and pepper. Roast for 30 minutes, turning halfway through cooking, or until the wedges are cooked through and browned at the edges (if the cabbage isn't browned enough for your taste, continue to cook for 5-minute increments until you're happy).

Meanwhile, to make the vinaigrette, whisk all the ingredients in a small bowl until combined.

When ready to serve, pile the cabbage wedges onto a serving platter and drizzle over the vinaigrette. Get stuck in immediately.

TIP *This is a delicious dish to take to work and enjoy cold. Any leftovers can be stored in an airtight container in the fridge for up to 5 days.*

ZESTY CHARGRILLED ZUCCHINI
with CURRIED CASHEW DIP

This recipe proves that delicious vegetables have their place on the barbie! This simple little combination of grilled zucchini and an Indian-inspired curried cashew dipping sauce is a perfect way to use up a glut of veg. It also makes a lovely addition to a vegan mezze meal.

SERVES 4

4 zucchini (a mix of different colours is lovely)
2 tablespoons extra-virgin olive or avocado oil
1 teaspoon ground coriander
1 teaspoon ground cumin
1 teaspoon chilli flakes
sea salt and freshly ground black pepper
coriander leaves, to serve

CURRIED CASHEW DIP

160 g (1 cup) cashew nuts, soaked in warm water for 1 hour or overnight, drained
zest and juice of 2 lemons
3 tablespoons extra-virgin olive, avocado, macadamia or hemp oil, plus extra if needed
2 garlic cloves, very finely chopped
1 teaspoon garam masala
½ teaspoon curry powder

For the cashew dip, blitz all the ingredients in a small food processor or blender until smooth (if you'd like a runnier dip, simply add an extra splash of oil or water). Set aside.

Heat a barbecue grill plate to very hot or place a chargrill pan over very high heat.

Cut the zucchini lengthways into halves or quarters, depending on their size. Add them to a bowl together with the olive oil, ground spices and chilli flakes, season well with salt and pepper and toss well to coat evenly.

Transfer the zucchini to the hot barbecue or pan and cook for 2–4 minutes, turning halfway through, until slightly soft and nicely charred on all sides (be careful not to overcook them as you don't want them super soft).

Pile the zucchini onto a serving platter and sprinkle over a few coriander leaves. Serve alongside the curried cashew dip.

HEALTH TIP *Zucchini contain high amounts of vitamin C and polyphenols, especially in the skin. Studies have found that the compounds in zucchini skin have positive effects on the thyroid and adrenal glands, with the compounds also helping to regulate insulin levels.*

SATAY JACKFRUIT SKEWERS

Young jackfruit is such a versatile ingredient – it is great as a substitute for meat in curries, burgers, tacos and souvlaki. Here it is stepping in as a delicious plant-based alternative to chicken. One bite of these skewers and this dish will become one of your new faves!

SERVES 4

600 g canned young jackfruit
 in water
sea salt and freshly ground
 black pepper
1 large handful of coriander leaves
1 lime, cut into wedges

MARINADE

2 tablespoons melted coconut oil
zest and juice of 2 limes
3 tablespoons coconut aminos
2 garlic cloves, finely diced
2 cm piece of ginger, peeled and
 finely grated
1 tablespoon ground turmeric
1 tablespoon maple syrup or
 coconut nectar (optional)

SATAY DIPPING SAUCE

150 g roasted peanuts
150 g peanut butter
2 tablespoons coconut aminos
 or tamari
3 cm piece of ginger, peeled and
 finely grated
1 long red chilli, deseeded and
 finely chopped
1 tablespoon extra-virgin olive,
 avocado, macadamia or hemp oil
1 tablespoon maple syrup or
 coconut nectar
125 ml (½ cup) filtered water, plus
 extra if needed
pinch of sea salt

Place eight bamboo skewers in a shallow dish, cover with cold water and leave to soak for at least 30 minutes.

Drain and rinse the jackfruit pieces really well. Using a sharp knife, cut off and discard any parts of the jackfruit that are hard or contain seeds (you want to try and use only the parts that are stringy or soft, as this will help to provide a similar texture to chicken).

Place all the marinade ingredients in a large bowl and whisk to combine. Add the jackfruit pieces and toss to coat, then cover and set aside in the fridge to marinate for at least 30 minutes (or up to 2 hours if you've got time).

For the satay dipping sauce, blitz all the ingredients in a food processor until smooth, adding an extra splash or two of water if the sauce is too thick. Set aside.

Heat a barbecue grill plate to medium or place a chargrill pan over medium heat.

Thread the marinated jackfruit cubes onto the prepared skewers and season well with salt and pepper. Cook the skewers, basting them with the marinade left behind in the bowl as you go, for about 3 minutes on each side, or until cooked through and nicely charred on the outside.

Transfer the cooked skewers to a serving platter, season with salt and pepper and scatter over the coriander leaves. Serve with the satay dipping sauce and some lime wedges for squeezing.

PORTOBELLO STEAKS *with* AVOCADO CHIMICHURRI

When I encourage people to eat more vegan food, the first thing I say to them is to start with real food. Ditch those faux meats, which can contain inflammatory ingredients, and stick with real fruits, vegetables, nuts, seeds and healthy, nutrient-dense fats. This recipe is a great embodiment of this real food philosophy.

SERVES 4

4 large portobello mushrooms, stalks removed
3 tablespoons balsamic vinegar
3 tablespoons extra-virgin olive, avocado, macadamia or hemp oil
½ teaspoon ground cumin
½ teaspoon sea salt
½ teaspoon freshly ground black pepper
¼ teaspoon smoked paprika
3 garlic cloves, very finely chopped

AVOCADO CHIMICHURRI
½ bunch of flat-leaf parsley, leaves finely chopped
3 garlic cloves, very finely chopped
¼ red onion, finely diced
½ teaspoon chilli flakes
3 tablespoons extra-virgin olive, avocado, macadamia or hemp oil
½ teaspoon sea salt
½ teaspoon freshly ground black pepper
zest and juice of 2 lemons
1 avocado, diced

Arrange the mushrooms in a shallow dish. Whisk together the balsamic vinegar, oil, cumin, salt, pepper, paprika and garlic in a bowl, then pour over the mushrooms. Leave to marinate for 10 minutes, turning the mushrooms halfway through to ensure they are evenly coated in the marinade.

Meanwhile, prepare the chimichurri. Add the parsley, garlic, onion, chilli flakes, oil, salt, pepper and lemon zest and juice to a bowl and whisk well. Add the avocado and toss to combine. Set aside.

Heat a barbecue grill plate to medium–hot or place a large chargrill pan over medium–high heat.

Transfer the mushrooms to the barbecue or pan and cook for 4–6 minutes, turning halfway through and brushing over any remaining marinade as you go, until they are caramelised and a deep golden brown.

To serve, divide the mushrooms among plates and top generously with the avocado chimichurri.

TIP *To take these steaks to the next level, try serving them on top of your favourite veggie mash (I love sweet potato or cauliflower).*

REALLY GOOD ROAST VEG
with SUMAC *and* DUKKAH

Gone are the days when roast vegetables meant just a tray of hot, crispy potatoes. Now, I am not saying there is anything wrong with that, but what I want to do here is get you thinking outside your comfort zone with the varieties of vegetables you use and how you go about jazzing them up. And if root vegetables really aren't your thing, keep in mind that you can totally try this with just potato and call it a day.

The dukkah here brings loads of flavour and texture to the veg, and can be made ahead of time. Keep the excess in an airtight container in the fridge for up to 1 week and experiment with it on your other favourite recipes – I like to sprinkle some over the broccoli steaks on page 47 or on many of the delicious salads in the Crispy and Crunchy chapter.

SERVES 4

1 large sweet potato
2 large carrots
2 parsnips, peeled
1 beetroot, peeled
½ swede, peeled
½ celeriac, peeled
1 red onion, unpeeled and
 quartered
1 garlic bulb, unpeeled and
 quartered
3 tablespoons extra-virgin olive
 or avocado oil
1 tablespoon sumac
2–3 thyme sprigs
2–3 rosemary sprigs
sea salt and freshly ground
 black pepper

DUKKAH (MAKES 100 G)
3 tablespoons sesame seeds
70 g (½ cup) pistachio kernels,
 finely chopped
3 teaspoons ground coriander
3 teaspoons ground cumin
½ teaspoon freshly ground
 black pepper
1 teaspoon sea salt

Preheat the oven to 220°C and line two large baking trays with baking paper.

Cut all the veg except the onion and garlic into 4 cm chunks. Transfer all the veg pieces including the onion and garlic to a large bowl and toss together with the oil and sumac, then spread them out evenly over the prepared trays. Scatter over the thyme and rosemary and bake for 45–50 minutes, or until the veg are golden brown and tender.

Meanwhile, for the dukkah, add the sesame seeds to a non-stick frying pan over medium heat. Cook, stirring, for 5 minutes, or until toasted and golden. Add the pistachios, ground spices and pepper and cook, stirring, for 1 minute, or until aromatic. Stir in the salt and set aside to cool.

Season the veg well with salt and pepper and sprinkle with a generous amount of the dukkah.

TIP *To peel or not to peel your veg, that is the question! I like to eat any veg peels that are clean, tender and tasty enough, as they contain good nutrients and fibre. Some vegetables like celeriac have a tough outer skin, which I always remove. Parsnips I assess on a case-by-case basis – the best flavour is actually right below the skin, so I try to avoid removing too much. As for carrots, I usually just scrub them well and leave the peel on.*

Just Like

THE REAL
THING

TOMATO, PESTO *and* OLIVE PIZZA
with BABY ROCKET

*I hope you absolutely LOVE this delicious pizza. It is so easy and I am particularly proud
of the crust. It's savoury, cheesy, crispy on the edges, tender in the centre and not to
mention really healthy and totally customisable. Oh, and it's also super tasty.
What are you waiting for?*

SERVES 4

1 tablespoon almond meal
1.2 kg (6 cups) raw Cauliflower
Rice (see page 125)
1½ Flax Eggs (see page 31)
¼ teaspoon sea salt
3 tablespoons Plant Parmesan (see
page 51) or nutritional yeast flakes
1 teaspoon chopped fresh
oregano or dried oregano
1 teaspoon chopped fresh basil or
dried basil
3 garlic cloves, very finely chopped
1 heaped tablespoon arrowroot
or tapioca flour

TOPPINGS

2 yellow tomatoes, finely sliced
3–4 red tomatoes, finely sliced
3 tablespoons pitted black olives,
halved
80 g (⅓ cup) Macadamia Pesto
(see page 70)
1 handful of baby rocket leaves
2 tablespoons extra-virgin olive oil

Preheat the oven to 190°C. Line a large baking tray or pizza tray
with baking paper and sprinkle over the almond meal (this will help
prevent the dough from sticking).

Make the cauliflower rice as instructed, then leave to cool. Once it
is cool enough to touch, pile it up in the centre of a clean tea towel,
gather the ends together, twist and firmly squeeze to remove any
excess liquid.

In a large bowl, prepare the flax eggs and leave them to rest for
5 minutes. Add the cauliflower rice, salt, plant parmesan or nutritional
yeast, oregano, basil, garlic and arrowroot or tapioca flour and stir
well or mix with your hands to combine. The mixture should be
dough-like in consistency; if not, add a little extra almond meal to
bring it together.

Using your hands, carefully spread the dough into a circle or square
depending on the shape of your prepared tray to a thickness of
about 1 cm, with a slightly thicker edge. Bake for 45 minutes, then
remove from the oven.

Carefully loosen the crust from the layer of paper with a spatula
and place another sheet of baking paper on top. Holding onto
both sheets of paper, gently flip the crust over, then return it to the
baking tray and remove the top layer of paper. Bake for an additional
10–12 minutes, or until the edge is golden brown and the centre feels
mostly firm to the touch. Remove from the oven and top with the
tomato slices and olives, then bake for another 10 minutes, or until
the tomatoes have collapsed a little. Serve topped with dollops of the
pesto, a scattering of baby rocket leaves and a drizzle of olive oil.

TIP *This pizza is best enjoyed fresh and eaten with a fork (I find
that it doesn't quite support itself when eaten with your hands). You
could bake your crust ahead of time and then freeze it for later use,
if desired. And, of course, you can top this with whatever you'd like
to add. This recipe calls for just a few simple ingredients, but you
can use whatever you've got on hand (the leftover roast vegetables
from page 112 are pretty great, too).*

LOADED SWEET POTATO FRIES *with* GUAC *and* CASHEW SOUR CREAM

I absolutely love these Mexican-inspired loaded sweet potato fries. Coating the fries in arrowroot or tapioca flour and giving them lots of space on the tray while baking are real game changers – you'll get perfectly crispy fries every time!

SERVES 4

2 large sweet potatoes (about 800 g in total)
40 g (⅓ cup) arrowroot or tapioca flour
1 teaspoon sea salt
2 tablespoons extra-virgin olive oil
2 tablespoons coriander leaves
1 lime, cut into cheeks, to serve (optional)

CASHEW SOUR CREAM (MAKES 250 G)
160 g (1 cup) cashew nuts, soaked for at least 15 minutes in hot water or 2 hours in cold water
juice of 1 lemon
2 teaspoons apple cider vinegar
½ teaspoon sea salt
80 ml (⅓ cup) filtered water

GUAC
1 avocado
zest and juice of 1 lime
1 tablespoon apple cider vinegar
1 teaspoon chilli flakes
½ teaspoon sea salt

Preheat the oven to 220°C and line two baking trays with baking paper.

Cut the sweet potatoes into evenly sized matchsticks, about 5 mm thick. Place in a bowl or sealable bag, add the arrowroot or tapioca flour and salt and toss or shake to coat evenly. Drizzle over the oil and toss or shake again.

Arrange the sweet potato matchsticks in a single layer over the prepared trays, leaving space between them. Bake for 15 minutes, then flip with a spatula and cook for a further 10–15 minutes, or until the fries are crispy and starting to turn brown in spots.

Meanwhile, make the cashew sour cream. Drain the soaked nuts and rinse them really well, then transfer to a high-speed blender or food processor with the remaining ingredients and blitz for 1–2 minutes, or until beautifully smooth.

To make the guac, mix all the ingredients in a bowl until well combined (you can make it as smooth or as chunky as you like).

Pile the sweet potato fries onto a large platter and top with generous dollops of the guac and cashew sour cream. Sprinkle over the coriander leaves, season well with salt and serve with the lime cheeks for squeezing, if you like.

TIP *Leftover cashew sour cream will keep stored in an airtight container in the fridge for up to 5 days (or frozen for up to 3 months) and is great dolloped over my Nice Nachos with Beetroot Chips (see page 144).*

PARSNIP SPAGHETTI
with SUNFLOWER BOLOGNESE

I absolutely love this recipe! I really enjoy the al dente mouthfeel from the parsnips, but feel free to swap them out and use any other of your favourite spiralised vegetables such as zucchini noodles or sweet potato noodles.

SERVES 4

3–4 parsnips, peeled
500 g (4 cups) cauliflower florets
60 g (½ cup) sunflower seeds
1 garlic clove, finely chopped
½ onion, roughly chopped
1 teaspoon dried mixed Italian
   herbs
1 tablespoon coconut oil
170 g can tomato paste
1 tablespoon balsamic vinegar
500 ml (2 cups) vegetable stock
   (see page 88 for homemade)
sea salt and freshly ground
   black pepper
Plant Parmesan (see page 51),
   to serve
1 handful of basil leaves, to serve

Using a mandoline, spiraliser or sharp knife, cut the parsnips into fine vegetable noodles. Set aside.

In a food processor, pulse together the cauliflower, sunflower seeds, garlic, onion and mixed herbs to form a rough, chunky paste.

Melt the coconut oil in a large non-stick frying pan over medium–high heat, add the cauliflower mixture and saute for 8–10 minutes, or until softened and lightly golden brown. Reduce the heat to medium, stir in the tomato paste, balsamic vinegar and vegetable stock and bring to a simmer. Cook for 10 minutes, stirring occasionally, until lovely and thick.

Meanwhile, cook the parsnip noodles in a saucepan of boiling salted water for 3–4 minutes, or until just tender, then drain and divide among bowls. To serve, spoon the bolognese over the noodles, season well with salt and pepper and scatter over the plant parmesan and a few basil leaves to finish. Enjoy.

HEALTH TIP *Sunflower seeds are rich in B vitamins, which are essential for a healthy nervous system, and are a good source of phosphorus, magnesium, iron, calcium, potassium, protein and vitamin E. They also contain zinc, manganese, copper, chromium and carotene as well as monounsaturated and polyunsaturated fatty acids – types of 'good' fat that may help to protect the arteries.*

HEMP and BEETROOT BURGERS with THE LOT

Mastering the art of the perfect meatless burger all came down to experimenting with delicious hemp seeds. They really hold this burger together and provide a lovely nutty texture, plus heaps of nutrition from all the healthy omega-3s and protein that's packed into them.

SERVES 4

55 g (⅓ cup) hulled hemp seeds, plus 3 tablespoons extra

175 g (⅔ cup) sunflower seeds, plus 3 tablespoons extra

2 beetroot, peeled and coarsly chopped

2 teaspoons onion powder

1 teaspoon sea salt

½ teaspoon freshly ground black pepper

1 teaspoon ground cumin

1 tablespoon ground coriander

1 heaped teaspoon dried parsley

1 tablespoon coconut cream

1 tablespoon arrowroot or tapioca flour

35 g (⅓ cup) almond meal

1–2 tablespoons filtered water, if needed

extra-virgin olive oil, for greasing

TO SERVE

1 butter lettuce, leaves separated

1 tomato, finely sliced

1 avocado, finely sliced

1 Lebanese cucumber, cut into ribbons

3 tablespoons Vegan Mayo (see page 52)

In a food processor, blitz the hemp and sunflower seeds to a coarse meal consistency. Add the beetroot, onion powder, salt, pepper, cumin, coriander and parsley and pulse for a few seconds to just bring everything together (it should be a little chunky, not a perfect puree – if you have a small food processor you might have to do this in batches).

Transfer the mixture to a large bowl and add the coconut cream, arrowroot or tapioca flour, almond meal and the extra hemp and sunflower seeds. Mix everything together with a spoon until evenly combined. The mixture should be really moist; if not, add a splash of water.

Heat a barbecue grill plate to medium–low or place a chargrill pan over medium–low heat. Lightly grease with olive oil.

Divide the hemp mixture into four even-sized portions and shape into patties. Cook for 8–10 minutes on each side, or until nicely charred and cooked through. (Take care when turning the patties over – they hold together well, but you can't be too rough with them either.)

To serve, pile a handful of lettuce leaves one inside the other to create a lettuce 'cup'. Repeat to make four cups. Pack each cup with the tomato and avocado, then top with a patty and some cucumber ribbons. Finish with a generous dollop of mayo and some extra salt and pepper. Get stuck in.

BROCCOLI MASALA *with* CAULIFLOWER RICE

I like to refer to this richly flavoured dish as a 'supermarket curry', because each and every ingredient is readily available at your local supermarket. That means there is no excuse not to whip this delicious meal up and get your kitchen smelling fantastic with its wonderful aromas.

SERVES 4

2 large sweet potatoes, cut into
   4 cm chunks
400 g can diced tomatoes
5 cm piece of ginger, peeled and
   roughly chopped
1 garlic clove, finely chopped
½ teaspoon sea salt
160 g (1 cup) macadamia nuts,
   toasted and crushed
2 tablespoons coconut oil
1 teaspoon chilli powder
1 teaspoon ground coriander
1 teaspoon ground cumin
½ teaspoon ground turmeric
500 ml (2 cups) vegetable stock
   (see page 88 for homemade)
250 ml (1 cup) coconut cream
1 cinnamon stick
1 large head of broccoli, cut into
   florets
2 tablespoons coriander leaves

CAULIFLOWER RICE (MAKES 800 G)
1 head of cauliflower (about 800 g),
   florets and stalk roughly chopped
2 tablespoons coconut oil
sea salt

Set a steamer basket over a saucepan of simmering water. Add the sweet potato, cover with a lid and steam for 10 minutes, or until tender and easily pierced with a fork. Drain and set aside.

Add the tomatoes, ginger, garlic, salt and half the macadamias to a food processor and blitz until smooth.

Melt the coconut oil in a heavy-based saucepan over medium heat. Add the chilli powder, ground coriander, cumin and turmeric and cook, stirring, for 1 minute, or until the spices are lovely and fragrant.

Pour the tomato mixture into the pan and cook, stirring, for 2–3 minutes. Add the stock, coconut cream and cinnamon stick and bring to the boil. Reduce the heat to a simmer and cook, uncovered and stirring occasionally, for 10 minutes, or until the sauce has reduced slightly. Add the sweet potato and broccoli, cover with a lid and simmer for a further 8 minutes, or until the broccoli is tender and the sauce has thickened up nicely.

Meanwhile, make the cauliflower rice. Place the chopped cauliflower in a food processor and pulse into tiny rice-like pieces (this usually takes six to eight pulses). Melt the coconut oil in a large frying pan over medium heat, add the cauliflower rice and saute for 4–6 minutes, or until softened. Season with salt to taste.

Remove the cinnamon stick from the curry and divide among bowls. Scatter over the coriander leaves and the remaining macadamias, and serve with the cauliflower rice.

Crispy ROSEMARY POTATO CAKES

It would be remiss of me not to include a potato cake recipe in this part of the book. (And as a Victorian, I do need to call them potato cakes, even if the rest of Australia might refer to them as scallops.) You see, anyone who knows me will understand why this recipe is so special to me – potato cakes are my thing. If someone asked what my last meal on earth would be, I'd say 12 potato cakes with salt, sauce and vinegar. It doesn't get much tastier or simpler.

SERVES 4

2 large coliban potatoes or other white floury potatoes
2 large sweet potatoes
125 ml (½ cup) coconut oil
sea salt
tomato sauce, to serve (optional)
BATTER
375 ml (1½ cups) filtered water
270 g (2¼ cups) arrowroot or tapioca flour
100 g (1 cup) almond meal
1½ tablespoons sea salt
1½ teaspoons dried rosemary

Get started by slicing the potatoes. Using a sharp knife, cut them on a slight angle into 7–10 mm thick ovals. Repeat with the sweet potatoes, trying to make them as equal as possible.

Lower the potato and sweet potato slices into a large saucepan of boiling water and cook for 2–3 minutes. Drain and spread out to cool.

While the potato slices cool, make the batter. Mix the water, arrowroot or tapioca flour, almond meal, salt and rosemary in a bowl to form a smooth batter. Transfer the batter to the fridge and leave for 5–10 minutes, or until the potato slices are cool enough to handle.

Heat the coconut oil in a large, heavy-based frying pan over medium–high heat until a bit of batter sizzles when dropped in. Working in batches, dip each potato slice into the prepared batter to coat well, let the excess drip off, then carefully lower into the oil and fry for 3–4 minutes on each side, or until golden brown all over. Transfer the cooked potato cakes to some paper towel to drain.

Serve the potato cakes straight away with a generous sprinkling of salt and some healthy tomato sauce, if you wish.

TIP *If you'd like to turn these into a healthy source of resistant starch, simply refrigerate or freeze them once you've finished frying, then re-fry or bake to reheat later on. If you are going to freeze them, to prevent them sticking together, spread them out on a chopping board for at least 2 hours before you stack them on top of each other in a container.*

NO-FUSS PLANT PAD THAI

You are going to love this quick and easy recipe, which takes just 30 minutes to prepare. Plus, check out all the colourful veggies you'll be eating! To replace the traditional rice noodles, I have gone with carrot 'noodles', greens, finely sliced red capsicum and red cabbage. Pad Thai has never looked so vibrant or delicious.

SERVES 4

1 tablespoon coconut oil
2 garlic cloves, very finely chopped
1 long red chilli, finely sliced
4 shallots, finely sliced
¼ small red cabbage, outer leaves discarded, finely sliced
1 red capsicum, finely sliced lengthways
2 tablespoons coconut aminos or tamari
4 carrots, cut into ribbons with a vegetable peeler
6 rainbow chard or kale leaves, stalks discarded, finely sliced
1 cm piece of ginger, peeled and finely grated
1 teaspoon grated fresh or ground turmeric

PEANUT SAUCE
3 tablespoons crunchy peanut butter
juice of 1½ limes, plus extra if needed
3 tablespoons coconut aminos or tamari, plus extra if needed
2 tablespoons maple syrup or coconut nectar, plus extra if needed
1 teaspoon chilli flakes, plus extra if needed

TO SERVE
1 handful of coriander leaves
2 tablespoons chopped roasted peanuts
1 teaspoon chilli flakes

To make the peanut sauce, whisk all the ingredients together in a small bowl. Taste and adjust the flavour as needed, adding more lime juice for acidity, coconut aminos for saltiness, dried chilli flakes for heat, or extra maple syrup for sweetness. Set aside.

Melt the coconut oil in a large frying pan over medium heat. Add the garlic, chilli, shallot, cabbage, capsicum and 1 tablespoon of the coconut aminos or tamari and cook, stirring frequently, for 3 minutes. Add the carrot, chard or kale and the remaining tablespoon of coconut aminos or tamari and saute for another 2–4 minutes. Add the peanut sauce, ginger and turmeric and cook, stirring often, for a further 3–4 minutes, or until everything is warmed through and the chard or kale is slightly wilted.

Remove from the heat and divide among serving plates. Serve, topped with the coriander, chopped peanuts and chilli flakes.

Cauli-mince Tacos

This super simple recipe delivers the flavours of Mexico in every mouthful. Once you make this cauliflower mince you will not look back – it is absolutely delicious and will have you returning for more each and every time.

SERVES 4

1 head of cauliflower, cut into florets
100 g (1 cup) pecans
2 bird's eye chillies, roughly chopped
2 teaspoons garlic powder
1 teaspoon onion powder
1 teaspoon ground cumin
1 teaspoon ground coriander
juice of 1 lime
sea salt and freshly ground black pepper
1 avocado
1 baby cos lettuce, leaves separated
1 teaspoon chilli flakes, to serve (optional)

Preheat the oven to 200°C and line two baking trays with baking paper.

Place the cauliflower, pecans, chilli, garlic and onion powders, cumin and coriander in a food processor and pulse six to eight times until well combined and finely chopped into small mince-like pieces. Transfer to a bowl, add half the lime juice, season with salt and mix well.

Spread the cauli-mince evenly over the prepared trays and roast in the oven for 30 minutes, stirring every 10 minutes, until golden brown and crisp.

Meanwhile, scoop the avocado flesh into a bowl and, using a fork, roughly smash with the remaining lime juice. Season with salt and pepper to taste.

To serve, pile a few lettuce leaves one inside the other to create a lettuce 'cup', then repeat with the remaining leaves to make eight cups. Spoon the cauli-mince into the cups, top with the smashed avo and sprinkle over some chilli flakes, if you like. Get eating.

TIP *When I use fresh chilli, I usually use the entire thing, seeds included. If you're not a fan of spicy food, simply remove the seeds for a milder heat.*

CRISPY ONION BHAJIS *with* CHILLI VEGAN MAYO

These crispy onion bhajis make the perfect snack or simple starter. They're light, crispy and completely more-ish! And jazzing up my easy vegan mayo with a few simple spices transforms it into the perfect accompaniment here.

SERVES 4

2 white onions
60 g (½ cup) arrowroot or tapioca flour
3 tablespoons almond meal
½ teaspoon gluten-free baking powder
1 teaspoon sea salt
1 teaspoon ground cumin
½ teaspoon ground turmeric
1 long red chilli, finely chopped
2 tablespoons finely chopped coriander leaves
1 teaspoon lemon juice
125 ml (½ cup) filtered water
coconut oil, for frying

CHILLI VEGAN MAYO

140 g (½ cup) Vegan Mayo (see page 52)
¼ teaspoon chilli powder
¼ teaspoon smoked paprika

For the chilli vegan mayo, stir the mayo, chilli powder and smoked paprika together in a bowl. Set aside.

Using a spiraliser, mandoline or sharp knife, spiralise or very finely slice the onions.

Place the arrowroot or tapioca flour, almond meal, baking powder, salt, cumin, turmeric, chilli, coriander and lemon juice in a large bowl and whisk to combine, then whisk in the water to create a lovely thick batter. Add the onion and, using your hands, mix well.

Preheat the oven to 100°C.

Heat a large, heavy-based frying pan over medium heat and fill with coconut oil to a depth of 1 cm. Heat the oil to 180°C. (To test if the oil is hot enough, simply drop a small piece of bread into it – if it sizzles and bubbles, you're good to go.) Carefully lower tablespoons of the bhaji mixture into the pan – about four bhajis per batch – and fry for 2 minutes, turning halfway through, until golden brown and crispy. Remove the bhajis with a slotted spoon and place on a plate lined with paper towel to drain. Transfer to the oven to keep warm and repeat with the remaining batter.

Divide the bhajis among plates or pile onto a serving platter, sprinkle with salt and serve with the chilli vegan mayo for dipping.

CAULIFLOWER POPCORN
with EASY BARBECUE SAUCE

This recipe takes cauliflower to the next level of awesome. In fact, it's so good that if you served it up at a kids' party, the little ones wouldn't even know they were eating veggies! The secret is the wonderful batter, which adds flavour and makes these popcorn pieces crispy and delicious. I recommend using a coconut, avocado or macadamia oil spray (which can be found in most supermarkets) to coat the popcorn pieces and deliver the crispiest results.

SERVES 4

100 g (1 cup) almond meal
2 teaspoons chilli powder
1 teaspoon garlic powder
2 teaspoons smoked paprika
2 teaspoons ground cumin
2 teaspoons ground turmeric
750 ml (3 cups) coconut cream
125 g (1 cup) arrowroot or
  tapioca flour
1 head of cauliflower, cut into
  bite-sized florets
coconut, avocado or macadamia
  oil spray or oil, for coating
sea salt and freshly ground
  black pepper

EASY BARBECUE SAUCE
3 tablespoons hulled tahini
75 g tomato paste
1 teaspoon maple syrup
¾ teaspoon garlic powder
1½ teaspoons apple cider vinegar
1½ teaspoons molasses
3 drops liquid smoke, or to taste
  (see Tip)
sea salt, to taste
½ teaspoon chilli powder
  (optional)
3 tablespoons filtered water, plus
  extra if needed

Preheat the oven to 180°C and line two large baking trays with baking paper.

Mix the almond meal, chilli powder, garlic powder, paprika, cumin and turmeric in a large bowl. In a separate large bowl, mix the coconut cream and arrowroot or tapioca flour to make a thick batter.

Dip a cauliflower floret briefly in the coconut cream batter to coat evenly, then toss it in the almond meal mixture. Transfer to a prepared tray and repeat with the rest of the florets.

When all the florets are ready, drizzle or give them a gentle spray with oil. Bake for 25–30 minutes, turning halfway and drizzling or re-spraying with oil if you wish, until golden brown and crisp.

Meanwhile, for the barbecue sauce, blitz all the ingredients in a food processor or high-speed blender until really smooth. If the sauce is a little thick, add an extra splash of water.

Remove the cauliflower popcorn pieces from the oven and season with salt and pepper to taste. Serve alongside the barbecue sauce.

TIP *Liquid smoke can be found in specialty food stores, some department stores and barbecue specialty stores. It is made from hickory, applewood or mesquite wood that is burned inside a chamber. As the smoke rises it is captured in a condenser and this cooled liquid smoke is then collected and filtered. Adding very small amounts of it to recipes gives them a wonderful smoky flavour, but be warned, a little goes a long way – the difference between using a little bit of it and going overboard is the difference between a sunny barbecue and a face full of smoke as the wind shifts.*

Sensational Souvlaki

Having grown up in Melbourne I feel like I know what a really good souvlaki tastes like (along with a good coffee, of course). Over the years I have certainly devoured some sensational souvlakis that have transported me to the streets of Greece with each and every mouthful, and I reckon this vegan version does the same. Don't believe me? Give it a try and see for yourself.

SERVES 4

800 g canned young jackfruit
  in water
3 tablespoons extra-virgin olive oil
1 red onion, finely diced
4 garlic cloves, finely diced
¼ teaspoon ground cinnamon
½ teaspoon ground cumin
2 teaspoons dried oregano
2 tablespoons tomato paste
3 tablespoons coconut aminos
  or tamari
2 tablespoons maple syrup or
  coconut nectar
2 teaspoons apple cider vinegar
¼ teaspoon freshly ground black
  pepper
1 teaspoon chilli powder (optional)

TZATZIKI
1 large Lebanese cucumber
250 g (1 cup) coconut yoghurt or
  coconut cream
3 garlic cloves, very finely chopped
1 small handful of dill fronds, finely
  chopped
zest and juice of 1 lemon
2 tablespoons extra-virgin olive,
  avocado, macadamia or hemp oil
sea salt, to taste

TO SERVE
4 Garlic Flatbreads (see page 60)
  or cos lettuce leaf 'cups'
12 cherry tomatoes, quartered
6 cos lettuce leaves, shredded
1 small Lebanese cucumber, halved
  and sliced
1 small red onion, very finely sliced
sea salt and freshly ground
  black pepper
lemon wedges

For the tzatziki, coarsely grate the cucumber by hand using a box grater or process in a food processor using the grater attachment. Wrap the grated cucumber in a clean tea towel and squeeze over a sink to remove as much excess liquid as possible, then add it to a large bowl together with the remaining ingredients. Mix everything well and refrigerate until needed.

Drain and rinse the jackfruit pieces really well. Using a sharp knife, cut off and discard any parts of the jackfruit that are hard or contain seeds (you want to try and use only the parts that are stringy or soft, as this will help to provide a similar texture to chicken).

Warm the olive oil in a heavy-based frying pan over medium–low heat, add the onion and garlic and saute for 3–4 minutes, or until softened and fragrant. Stir in the cinnamon, cumin, oregano and tomato paste and cook for a further 2–3 minutes. Add the jackfruit, coconut aminos or tamari, sweetener and vinegar. Mix everything really well and, using the back of your spoon, squash the jackfruit pieces slightly. Add the pepper and chilli powder (if using), bring to a gentle simmer and cook for another 10–15 minutes, or until the sauce is lovely and sticky. Remove from the heat.

Preheat the oven to 200°C and line a baking tray with baking paper.

Once cool, spread the jackfruit mixture onto the prepared tray, transfer to the oven and cook for 20–25 minutes, or until the jackfruit pieces are slightly caramelised and beginning to brown around the edges.

To serve, arrange your flatbreads or lettuce leaf 'cups' on a platter and top with the tomato, shredded lettuce and sliced cucumber and onion. Spoon over the baked jackfruit, dollop on the tzatziki, season with salt and pepper and enjoy with some lemon wedges for squeezing.

CRISPY EGGPLANT KATSU CURRY

With its crispy coconut coating and rich curry sauce, this vegan version of the popular Japanese dish ticks all the taste and health boxes for me. This recipe is inspired by childhood days spent walking past my local Japanese takeaway shop after school and picking up a bento box that always included katsu curry. It was by far my favourite part of the day.

SERVES 4

2 eggplants, cut lengthways into 1 cm thick slices
2 teaspoons sea salt
60 g (½ cup) arrowroot or tapioca flour
3 tablespoons coconut flour
1½ tablespoons ground flaxseeds
200 ml filtered water
3 tablespoons coconut cream
90 g (1 cup) desiccated coconut
170 g (1 cup) hemp seeds
3 tablespoons sesame seeds
2 teaspoons garlic powder
coconut oil, for deep-frying
800 g (4 cups) Cauliflower Rice (see page 125), cooked, to serve

CURRY SAUCE

1 tablespoon coconut oil
1 small onion, finely chopped
4 garlic cloves, very finely chopped
1 tablespoon curry powder
1 tablespoon arrowroot or tapioca flour
375 ml (1½ cups) vegetable stock (see page 88 for homemade)
2 tablespoons coconut aminos or tamari
1 tablespoon apple cider vinegar
1 tablespoon maple syrup or coconut nectar

SALAD

¼ small green cabbage, outer leaves discarded, finely shredded
¼ small red cabbage, outer leaves discarded, finely shredded
2 spring onions, finely sliced diagonally, plus extra to serve
1 tablespoon apple cider vinegar
1 teaspoon maple syrup or coconut nectar

Arrange the eggplant slices on two trays in a single layer. Sprinkle over the salt and set aside for 20 minutes.

Meanwhile, make the curry sauce. Heat the coconut oil in a small saucepan over medium–high heat. Add the onion, garlic and curry powder and cook, stirring, for 3–4 minutes, or until the onion is softened. Stir in the arrowroot or tapioca flour, then gradually pour in the stock, stirring constantly, until fully incorporated. Add the coconut aminos or tamari, vinegar and sweetener and bring to a simmer. Cook for 5–10 minutes, stirring occasionally, until slightly thickened. Remove from the heat and leave to cool slightly, then transfer to a food processor and blitz until smooth. Set aside.

Combine the arrowroot or tapioca flour and coconut flour in a shallow bowl. In a separate bowl, whisk together the ground flaxseeds, water and coconut cream. In a third bowl, combine the desiccated coconut, hemp seeds, sesame seeds and garlic powder and mix well.

Using paper towel, wipe the salt from the eggplant slices and pat dry. Place an eggplant slice in the flour mixture and turn to coat, shaking off the excess. Next, dip it in the flaxseed mixture and finally in the coconut and hemp seed mixture, pressing down lightly to secure the crumb. Transfer to a plate and set aside. Repeat with the remaining eggplant slices until they are all coated.

Heat a large, heavy-based frying pan over medium heat and fill with the coconut oil to a depth of 1 cm. Heat the oil to 180°C. (To test if the oil is hot enough, simply drop a small piece of bread into it – if it sizzles and bubbles, you're good to go.) Add half the eggplant slices and cook for 4–5 minutes on each side, or until golden. Carefully remove the eggplant and drain on paper towel. Repeat with the remaining eggplant slices.

To make the salad, add the green and red cabbage and spring onion to a bowl, drizzle over the vinegar and sweetener and toss to combine.

When ready to serve, reheat the curry sauce in a saucepan over medium heat. Divide the salad and cauliflower rice among plates, top with the eggplant, drizzle over the warm curry sauce and sprinkle over a little extra spring onion.

SALT *and* PEPPER PALM HEARTS

Palm hearts, or hearts of palm, can be found canned in most major supermarkets and Asian grocers. They bear an uncanny resemblance to calamari, making them perfect for this crispy salt and pepper recipe.

SERVES 4

1.6 kg canned palm hearts
125 g (1 cup) arrowroot or tapioca flour
3 tablespoons almond meal
3 tablespoons coconut flour
1 tablespoon sea salt
1 tablespoon ground white pepper
coconut oil, for frying
lime wedges, to serve

CHILLI SAUCE
pinch of sea salt
2 garlic cloves, very finely chopped
1 long red chilli, deseeded and finely chopped
1 spring onion, finely sliced
1 teaspoon maple syrup or coconut nectar
2 tablespoons coconut aminos or tamari
2 tablespoons extra-virgin olive or avocado oil

BATTER
125 g (1 cup) arrowroot or tapioca flour
100 ml coconut cream
100 ml iced filtered water

To make the chilli sauce, mash the salt and garlic together in a bowl. Add the remaining ingredients and whisk well. Set aside.

Drain the canned palm hearts, then pat them dry with paper towel and cut into 2 cm thick discs. Using your fingers, carefully push out the centre from each disc (these can be blended together with other vegetables to create a delicious dip, or used to bulk out soups).

Mix the arrowroot or tapioca flour, almond meal, coconut flour and salt and pepper in a shallow bowl. Add the palm hearts and toss them through the crumb mixture to coat well. (Alternatively, place the ingredients in a resealable bag, add the palm heart discs and shake well.)

For the batter, whisk together the arrowroot or tapioca flour, coconut cream and iced water in a bowl.

Heat a large, heavy-based frying pan over medium heat and fill with coconut oil to a depth of 2.5 cm. Heat the oil to 180°C. (To test if the oil is hot enough, simply drop a small piece of bread into it – if it sizzles and bubbles, you're good to go.)

Working in batches, dip the crumb-coated palm heart discs in the batter, then dip into the salt and pepper crumb again. Once coated, lower them into the hot oil – do not overcrowd the pan – and fry for 3–4 minutes, turning halfway through cooking, until golden brown all over. Once cooked, remove from the pan and place on paper towel to drain.

Pile the salt and pepper palm hearts onto a platter and serve with the chilli sauce and lime wedges.

HEALTH TIP *Palm heart is a delicious, crunchy vegetable harvested from the centre of the cabbage palm tree. Though it resembles white asparagus, the flavour is much more delicate, making it extremely versatile in cooking (when finely chopped it breaks into shreds that resemble fresh crab meat, making it perfect for salads, stir-fries and dips). Nutritionally speaking, palm heart is also an excellent source of protein and fibre, as well as potassium, vitamins B6 and C, calcium, niacin, phosphorus and zinc.*

Tempura Tacos

*Tempura and tacos are two of my favourite 'T' words. And when you put them together ...
well, the only word left for them is INCREDIBLE. I love how delicious and crispy this batter
is, and the eggplant really shines in this recipe. Feel free to mix up the fillings and sauces
with anything else you've already made in bulk or have on hand.*

SERVES 4

I eggplant, peeled and cut into
   8 cm x 2 cm batons
I teaspoon sea salt
coconut oil, for deep-frying
60 g (½ cup) arrowroot or
   tapioca flour, for dusting

TORTILLAS
100 g (1 cup) almond meal
125 g (1 cup) arrowroot or
   tapioca flour
180 ml (¾ cup) coconut milk
½ teaspoon sea salt
125 ml (½ cup) filtered water
pinch of ground turmeric
2–3 tablespoons coconut oil

TEMPURA BATTER
200 ml filtered water
200 g arrowroot or tapioca flour
I teaspoon sea salt

TO SERVE
¼ iceberg lettuce, shredded
I avocado, sliced
140 g (½ cup) Vegan Mayo (see
   page 52)
juice of I lime
I handful of coriander leaves,
   roughly torn

Place the eggplant in a colander set over a plate and sprinkle over the salt. Leave for 30 minutes to draw out moisture, then rinse and pat dry with paper towel.

Preheat the oven to 100°C.

To make the tortillas, blitz all the ingredients except the coconut oil in a food processor or high-speed blender to form a smooth batter. Melt a little of the coconut oil in a large frying pan over medium–low heat. Pour in 60 ml (¼ cup) of the batter and smooth out into a thin round shape with a spatula or spoon. Cook for 1–2 minutes until sturdy enough to flip, then cook for a further 1–2 minutes on the other side until cooked through, puffed up and golden. Transfer the cooked tortilla to a plate in the oven to keep warm. Repeat this process with the remaining batter, adding a little more oil each time, to make eight tortillas.

To make the tempura batter, whisk all the ingredients together in a large bowl until smooth.

Half-fill a large, heavy-based saucepan with coconut oil and place over medium heat. Heat the oil to 180°C. (To test if the oil is hot enough, simply drop a small piece of bread into it – if it sizzles and bubbles, you're good to go.)

Add the arrowroot or tapioca flour to a shallow bowl. Working in batches, lightly coat the eggplant first in the arrowroot or tapioca flour and then in the batter. Immediately lower the coated eggplant, one at a time, into the hot oil and deep-fry for 4 minutes, or until golden and very crispy. Remove from the pan using a slotted spoon and transfer to a plate lined with paper towel to drain. Repeat with the remaining eggplant, being sure to bring the oil back up to temperature between batches.

To serve, divide the tortillas among plates and top each with the crispy tempura eggplant. Add some shredded iceberg and avo, a drizzle of mayo, a squeeze of lime juice and a scattering of coriander. Wrap, eat and repeat.

NICE NACHOS
with BEETROOT CHIPS

As you know, I like to make things from scratch. So, rather than using packet corn chips, I've done a little thinking outside the square and opted for colourful beetroot chips instead. Using beetroot adds so much vibrancy to the plate that just looking at this dish makes me happy.

SERVES 4

3 large beetroot, rinsed and
   scrubbed
olive or avocado oil or oil spray
sea salt and freshly ground
   black pepper

AVOCADO CREAM

2 avocados
2 tablespoons coconut cream
2 teaspoons extra-virgin olive,
   avocado, macadamia or hemp oil
zest and juice of 1 lime
sea salt and freshly ground black
   pepper, to taste

SPICY TOMATO SALSA

4 tomatoes, finely diced
½ red onion, finely diced
1 bunch of coriander, leaves
   roughly chopped, plus extra
   to serve
1 long red chilli, finely chopped
zest and juice of 1 lime
2 tablespoons extra-virgin olive,
   avocado, macadamia or hemp oil
sea salt and freshly ground black
   pepper, to taste

MACADAMIA CHEESE

160 g (1 cup) macadamia nuts,
   soaked in water for 1 hour,
   drained
125 ml (½ cup) filtered water
½ teaspoon sea salt
zest and juice of 1 lemon

Preheat the oven to 190°C and place an oven rack in the centre of the oven. Line two baking trays with baking paper.

Using a mandoline or sharp knife, slice the beetroot as finely as possible (they should curl a little when cut). Divide the slices between the prepared trays and spray or very lightly drizzle with the oil, season with salt and pepper and toss well to coat. Arrange the coated slices in a single layer, making sure there is space between each slice for ultimate crispiness, and bake for 15–20 minutes, or until crispy and slightly brown. (Be sure to watch the chips closely past the 15-minute mark as they can burn quickly.) Remove from the oven and set aside to cool while you prepare the other elements.

To make the avocado cream, blitz the ingredients in a food processor until smooth. Cover and keep in the fridge until needed.

For the tomato salsa, combine all the ingredients in a bowl. Set aside.

To make the macadamia cheese, blitz all the ingredients in the food processor until smooth and creamy.

When ready to serve, spread the beetroot chips out on a platter. Dollop over spoonfuls of the avocado cream, salsa and macadamia cheese and sprinkle over a little extra chopped coriander to finish.

'KFJ'
(KENTUCKY FRIED JACKFRUIT)

You'll see I have used the ever-versatile jackfruit in this book whenever I have needed to replicate anything fleshy and hearty (in particular, the mouthfeel and texture of chicken). This vegan take on Kentucky Fried Chicken tastes so close to the original you'll be triple checking what ingredients you used. Fantastic for entertaining and a real crowd pleaser, I know this will become a new favourite in your house.

SERVES 4

540 g canned young jackfruit
   in water
coconut oil, for frying
sea salt and freshly ground
   black pepper
Vegan Mayo (see page 52), to serve

BUTTERMILK

250 ml (1 cup) coconut milk
1½ tablespoons apple cider
   vinegar

CRUMB

140 g arrowroot or tapioca flour
50 g (½ cup) almond meal
1½ teaspoons sea salt
1 teaspoon freshly ground black
   pepper
1 teaspoon onion powder
1 teaspoon dried thyme
1 teaspoon dried oregano
1 teaspoon ground ginger
1 teaspoon smoked paprika
1 teaspoon garlic powder
½ teaspoon cayenne pepper
½ teaspoon chilli flakes (optional)

Combine the buttermilk ingredients in a large bowl. Set aside.

In a second large bowl, combine the crumb ingredients. Set aside.

Drain and rinse the jackfruit pieces really well. Using a sharp knife, cut off and discard any parts of the jackfruit that are hard or contain seeds (you want to try to use only the parts that are stringy or soft, as this will help to provide a similar texture to chicken).

Dip the trimmed jackfruit pieces first in the buttermilk, then in the crumb, then return to the buttermilk before finally dipping in the crumb mixture once again.

Place a large, heavy-based frying pan over medium heat and fill with coconut oil to a depth of 2.5 cm. Heat the oil to 180°C. (To test if the oil is hot enough, simply drop a small piece of bread into it – if it sizzles and bubbles, you're good to go.) Add the crumbed jackfruit in batches, being careful not to overcrowd the pan. Fry for 4–6 minutes, turning halfway through, until golden brown and crispy. Once cooked, remove with a slotted spoon and place on paper towel to drain.

Pile the jackfruit pieces onto a platter, season well with salt and pepper and serve with the vegan mayo for dipping. Enjoy!

TREATY
EATS

Luke's Chocolate

As you guys might know by now, I am a huge chocolate lover, especially when that chocolate is made from scratch. I have refined and revised this recipe many times over the years to get it to the perfect consistency and flavour. It is fantastic as a snack, or used in my other recipes that call for melted chocolate or chocolate chips. Feel free to have a go tweaking it to your liking, too, with some of my suggestions below.

MAKES ABOUT 500 G

220 g (1 cup) cacao butter, plus extra if needed

125 ml (½ cup) coconut oil, plus extra if needed

125 g (½ cup) smooth peanut butter or macadamia nut butter, plus extra if needed

250 g (2 cups) cacao powder, plus extra if needed

1 teaspoon vanilla bean paste or powder

2–4 drops liquid stevia or 250 ml (1 cup) monk fruit syrup, maple syrup or coconut nectar

Line a baking tray or brownie tin with baking paper, or a standard 12-hole muffin tin with paper cases.

In a saucepan over medium–low heat, gently stir together the cacao butter and coconut oil until melted. Add the nut butter and heat, stirring frequently, for 3–4 minutes, or until the nut butter has softened and is completely incorporated into the mixture.

Remove the pan from the heat and gently whisk in the cacao powder, vanilla and your sweetener of choice. Keep whisking until thick, creamy and well combined, then taste and adjust the consistency and sweetness as follows:

For a thicker, darker chocolate, add some more cacao powder.

For a smoother chocolate, add some more coconut oil.

For a fudgy chocolate, add some more nut butter.

For a sweeter chocolate, add some more sweetener of choice.

Once the chocolate is to your desired taste and consistency, pour it into your prepared tray or tin, transfer to the fridge or freezer and leave until set firm. Store in a suitable airtight container in the fridge for up to 1 month or in the freezer for up to 3 months.

TIP *You'll see that any recipe that calls for chocolate in this book uses this chocolate recipe. The reason for this is that, not only is it really good for you, it's also a great recipe to make in bulk and have on hand for when you want to get creative. If you really don't have time to make it, though, you can always swap it out for a good-quality dark chocolate with 90% cocoa solids.*

CAULIFLOWER COOKIES
and CREAM

Who said treats have to be unhealthy? One thing you'll notice with all my dessert recipes is that I do my best to increase nutrient density, decrease sugar content and keep you feeling fuller for longer. This allows you to reset your cravings, reduce over-eating and become an intuitive eater. Adding cauliflower rice to your cookies is another great way to celebrate vegetables, adding extra nutrients to each and every sweet mouthful.

MAKES 24 COOKIES

400 g (2 cups) raw Cauliflower Rice (see page 125)

125 ml (½ cup) melted coconut oil

125 ml (½ cup) maple syrup, coconut nectar or monk fruit syrup

1 teaspoon vanilla bean paste or powder

180 g (2 cups) desiccated coconut

150 g (1½ cups) almond meal

2 tablespoons arrowroot or tapioca flour, plus extra for dusting

1 tablespoon hemp seeds

pinch of sea salt

WHIPPED COCONUT CREAM

400 ml can coconut cream, refrigerated upside-down overnight

1–2 drops liquid stevia, plus extra if needed

½ teaspoon vanilla bean paste or powder

Preheat the oven to 180°C and line two large baking trays with baking paper. Place a large mixing bowl in the fridge to chill.

In a food processor or using a hand-held blender, blitz together the cauliflower rice, coconut oil, sweetener and vanilla until well combined, smooth and creamy. Add the remaining ingredients and stir well to form a dough.

Dust a chopping board or piece of baking paper with a little extra arrowroot or tapioca flour and scoop a tablespoon of the dough out onto it. Using your hands, roll the dough into a ball, then transfer to one of the prepared trays and flatten to a thickness of about 5 mm. Repeat with the remainder of your cookie dough, leaving about 2 cm between each cookie. Transfer the trays to the oven and bake for 20–25 minutes, or until the cookies are golden brown. Leave them to cool slightly on the trays, then transfer to a wire rack to cool.

While the cookies are cooling, make your whipped coconut cream. Remove both the chilled bowl and the can of coconut cream from the fridge, taking care not to shake the can as you go. Scoop the solid set coconut cream from the can into the bowl, being careful not to add any of the clear coconut liquid (keep this for using in smoothies, sauces and curries). Using a hand-held blender, blitz for 30 seconds, then add the stevia and vanilla and blitz for a further minute, or until creamy and smooth. Taste and adjust the sweetness by adding more stevia if needed.

Serve your cookies alongside the whipped coconut cream for dipping.

TIP *These cookies will keep stored in an airtight container in the fridge for 1 week or in the freezer for 3 months. The cream can be kept in an airtight container in the fridge for up to 2 weeks, though it will harden and set the longer it's chilled – to bring it back to its whipped consistency, just give it another quick blitz with a hand-held blender.*

DOUBLE CHOC ESPRESSO BROWNIES

Does the world really need another brownie recipe? Yes, it does! Especially when these are pretty much the equivalent of chocolate truffles in brownie form. And no matter whether you like your brownie soft and gooey or cakey and chewy, I have you covered with timing options that are guaranteed to deliver the perfect bite every time.

MAKES 12 BROWNIES

coconut oil, for greasing
75 g (¾ cup) almond meal
2 tablespoons arrowroot or tapioca flour
40 g (⅓ cup) cacao powder
1 teaspoon gluten-free baking powder
½ teaspoon sea salt
150 g (1 cup) roughly chopped Luke's Chocolate (see page 150), plus extra, grated, to serve
125 ml (½ cup) hot espresso coffee
1 teaspoon vanilla bean paste or powder
125 g (½ cup) peanut or almond butter
125 ml (½ cup) maple syrup, coconut nectar or monk fruit syrup
Whipped Coconut Cream (see page 153), to serve (optional)

Preheat the oven to 180°C and line the base and sides of a 20 cm square baking tin with baking paper. Lightly grease the baking paper with some coconut oil.

Add the almond meal, arrowroot or tapioca flour, cacao powder, baking powder and salt to a bowl and whisk well to combine.

Add half the chocolate to a separate bowl and pour over the hot coffee. Leave for 1 minute to allow the chocolate to soften and start to melt, then whisk well. Add the vanilla, nut butter and your sweetener of choice and whisk again to bring everything together.

Tip the dry ingredients into the wet ingredients, whisking vigorously for 1–2 minutes to form a smooth, lump-free batter. Stir in the remaining chocolate chunks, then spoon the batter into the prepared tin and spread it out in a thin, even layer.

For fudgy brownies, bake for 16–18 minutes, or until the centre of the brownie still looks soft but the edges are firm. Remove from the oven and leave to cool in the tin for at least 1 hour before removing and cutting into pieces. (These softer brownies can be harder to remove from the pan in one piece.)

For chewy, cakey brownies, bake for 20–22 minutes, or until the brownie is firm all over and the surface is flaky and cracked. Remove from the oven and leave to cool for 5–10 minutes before removing from the tin. These brownies are easier to remove in one piece.

Serve the brownies as they come, or with a dollop of my whipped coconut cream, if you like, and a sprinkle of grated chocolate. Any leftover brownies (is there such a thing?) will keep stored in an airtight container at room temperature for up to 5 days, or in the freezer for up to 1 month.

Coconut Banana Fritters

It doesn't get much better than this flavour combo of banana, coconut and caramel. It's like a tropical island vacation in each and every mouthful. If you want to take these awesome fritters to the next level, try melting down some of my chocolate (see page 150) and drizzling it over the top. Enjoy, legends!

SERVES 4

100 g (1 cup) almond meal
185 g (1½ cups) arrowroot or tapioca flour
½ teaspoon bicarbonate of soda
500 ml (2 cups) soda water
90 g (1 cup) desiccated coconut
65 g (½ cup) coconut flour
coconut oil, for frying
4 large bananas, peeled and cut into quarters
1 teaspoon vanilla powder
1 teaspoon ground cinnamon

CARAMEL SAUCE

400 ml can coconut cream, refrigerated upside-down overnight
250 ml (1 cup) maple syrup, coconut nectar or monk fruit syrup
1 teaspoon vanilla bean paste or powder

To make the caramel sauce, remove the can of coconut cream from the fridge, taking care not to shake the can as you go. Scoop 125 ml (½ cup) of the solid set coconut cream from the can into a saucepan, being careful not to add any of the clear coconut liquid (keep this for using in smoothies, sauces and curries). Add the remaining ingredients to the pan, place over medium heat and stir for 4–5 minutes, or until smooth. Bring to a simmer, then reduce the heat to low and leave to bubble away for 4–5 minutes until thickened up nicely. Remove from the heat and set aside.

Combine the almond meal, 125 g (1 cup) of the arrowroot or tapioca flour and the bicarb in a bowl, pour over the soda water and mix to form a batter.

Put the remaining arrowroot or tapioca flour in a shallow bowl.

In a separate shallow bowl, combine the desiccated coconut and coconut flour.

Half-fill a large, heavy-based saucepan with coconut oil over medium heat. Heat the oil to 180°C. (To test if the oil is hot enough, simply drop a small piece of bread into it – if it sizzles and bubbles, you're good to go.)

Roll three pieces of banana in the arrowroot flour and shake off the excess, then dip into the batter and roll in the coconut crumb to coat. Carefully lower the banana into the hot oil and cook for 1–2 minutes, or until golden brown. Remove with a slotted spoon, transfer to a plate lined with paper towel and repeat, in batches of three, until all the banana has been cooked.

Divide the fritters among plates or pile them onto a serving platter. Dust them with the vanilla powder and cinnamon and serve with the caramel sauce.

HEALTH TIP *When it comes to desserts, there isn't always a way to make them lower carb, especially when using the goodness of fresh fruit. That said, using monk fruit syrup here instead of maple syrup or coconut nectar will help reduce the overall sugar load of this recipe. (For more info on sweeteners, see page 13.)*

APPLE *and* BERRY COCONUT CRUMBLE

There's something sensational about the combination of toasted nuts and oven-baked fruit; you get that incredible soft texture from the fruit along with that fantastic crunch when the spoon digs into the nut crumble. This recipe calls for apples, blueberries and blackberries, but do try and experiment here (pears and strawberries also work well).

SERVES 4-6

4 green apples, cored and cut into 2 cm cubes
1 teaspoon vanilla bean paste or powder
1 teaspoon ground cinnamon
½ teaspoon ground nutmeg
2 tablespoons filtered water
155 g (1 cup) blueberries, fresh or frozen and thawed
155 g (1 cup) blackberries, fresh or frozen and thawed
Whipped Coconut Cream (see page 153), to serve

COCONUT CRUMBLE

100 g (1 cup) almond meal
3 tablespoons coconut oil, chilled
160 g (1 cup) macadamia nuts, roughly chopped
3 tablespoons shredded coconut
2 tablespoons pecans, roughly chopped
2 tablespoons hemp seeds
2 tablespoons maple syrup, coconut nectar or monk fruit syrup

Preheat the oven to 180°C.

Arrange the apple in a large baking dish and sprinkle over the vanilla, cinnamon, nutmeg and water. Cover with foil and bake for 20 minutes, or until the apple is soft, but still very much holding its shape. Remove from the oven, uncover and set aside.

For the coconut crumble, mix the almond meal and cold coconut oil in a bowl with your fingertips until the mixture resembles fine breadcrumbs. Add the macadamia nuts, shredded coconut, pecans and hemp seeds and mix well, then stir in your sweetener of choice.

Dot the blueberries and blackberries evenly over the par-cooked apples and, using your hands, spread the crumble mixture over the top, making sure it covers everything evenly and there are no gaps.

Bake the crumble in the oven for 10–15 minutes, or until the topping is crunchy and golden. Serve warm with the whipped coconut cream.

HEALTH TIP *There's an argument to be made for calling blackberries a superfood. They are high in beneficial vitamins and minerals, fibre and antioxidants, not to mention being really versatile and easy to add to your diet. What's not to love?*

THE ULTIMATE CHOCOLATE MOUSSE
with TOASTED HAZELNUT CRUMB

I absolutely LOVE chocolate mousse in all its forms. In fact, the first recipe I cracked when practising for my My Kitchen Rules debut back in 2012 was a mousse just like this. My goal was to pack as many fruits and vegetables into it as possible without anyone being able to tell. I think, after all these years, I have officially mastered it.

SERVES 4–6

500 ml (2 cups) coconut cream, plus extra if needed

1 large avocado

115 g (½ cup) Pumpkin Puree (see page 18) (optional)

250 g (2 cups) cacao powder

1 teaspoon vanilla bean paste or powder

2–4 drops liquid stevia or 125 ml (½ cup) maple syrup, coconut nectar or monk fruit syrup, plus extra if needed

70 g (½ cup) hazelnuts, skins removed

Whipped Coconut Cream (see page 153), to serve (optional)

Place the coconut cream, avocado flesh and pumpkin puree (if using) in a food processor and blitz until completely smooth. Add the cacao powder, vanilla and your sweetener of choice and blitz again to incorporate. Check for consistency and sweetness – adding a dash more coconut cream if it's a little thick and a little extra sweetener if needed. Blitz again until smooth and creamy, transfer to a bowl, then cover and place in the fridge until ready to serve. (This can be done in advance and the mousse kept in an airtight container for a day or two before serving.)

When ready to eat, toast the hazelnuts in a frying pan over medium–high heat for 2–3 minutes, or until golden brown and aromatic, shaking the pan to move them around as you go so they don't burn. Remove from the heat and set aside to cool slightly, then wrap them in a clean tea towel and crush them with a rolling pin to a rough crumb.

Serve your mousse topped with the toasted hazelnut crumb and a dollop of whipped coconut cream, if you wish.

TIRAMISU *in a* JAR

These single-serve tiramisu jars are great for when you're entertaining as well as being the perfect snacks to have on hand. All of the elements can be made ahead of time (and in larger quantities if necessary), and then put together when it's time to serve.

SERVES 4

3 tablespoons espresso, cold
4 tablespoons cacao powder, plus
  extra to sprinkle
Luke's Chocolate (see page 150),
  coarsely grated, to serve
  (optional)

SPONGE

100 g (1 cup) almond meal
125 g (1 cup) arrowroot or
  tapioca flour
3 tablespoons coconut sugar
½ teaspoon gluten-free baking
  powder
¼ teaspoon bicarbonate of soda
1 tablespoon apple cider vinegar
125 ml (½ cup) coconut milk
125 ml (½ cup) melted coconut oil
1 teaspoon vanilla bean paste
  or powder

COFFEE CREAM

200 g (1¼ cups) cashew nuts,
  soaked in water for 2 hours,
  drained
125 ml (½ cup) espresso, cold
3 tablespoons maple syrup,
  coconut nectar or monk
  fruit syrup
2 tablespoons coconut cream
2 teaspoons melted coconut oil

COCONUT CREAM

4 x 400 ml cans coconut cream,
  refrigerated upside-down
  overnight
2 tablespoons maple syrup,
  coconut nectar or monk
  fruit syrup
1 teaspoon vanilla bean paste
  or powder

Preheat the oven to 180°C and line a 20 cm x 30 cm baking tin with baking paper.

To make the sponge, add the dry ingredients to a large bowl and mix well to combine. In a separate bowl, whisk the wet ingredients. Add the wet ingredients to the dry ingredients and mix everything well to form a batter. Pour the batter into the prepared tin and bake for 15–20 minutes, or until light golden brown and a skewer inserted in the centre comes out clean. Set aside to cool completely.

For the coffee cream, place all the ingredients in a food processor or high-speed blender and blitz until smooth. (You may need to stop and scrape down the side with a spatula a few times to ensure everything gets mixed well.) Refrigerate until needed.

For the coconut cream, remove the cans of coconut cream from the fridge, taking care not to shake the cans as you go. Scoop the solid set coconut cream from the cans into the bowl of a food processor or high-speed blender, being careful not to add any of the clear coconut liquid (keep this for using in smoothies, sauces and curries). Add the remaining ingredients and blitz until smooth and fluffy. (Be mindful not to over-blend here as you will lose the fluffiness.) Transfer to the fridge until needed.

When you are ready to eat, take four 375 ml (1½ cup) capacity jars, clear ramekins or glasses and cut four circles out of the sponge to a size that matches the base of your vessels. Begin layering your tiramisu jars by placing a sponge circle in the bottom of each. Pour a few teaspoons of coffee over the sponge circles to soak slightly, then layer over half the coffee cream followed by half the coconut cream. Sprinkle with 1 tablespoon of cacao powder and repeat the layers, starting with four sponge circles and finishing with a final sprinkling of cacao powder and some grated chocolate, if desired.

SALTED PEANUT *and* CHOCOLATE TART

You're probably able to spot a few of my favourite ingredients by now, especially when it comes to this dessert chapter, where cacao, peanuts and coconut cream all get a good workout. Together, in my eyes, they are a flavour match made in heaven and here they combine to make this super easy – and wonderfully delicious – tart. Whip it up yourself and you'll be the talk of the town, I guarantee it.

SERVES 12

135 ml coconut cream

115 g Luke's Chocolate (see page 150), roughly chopped

140 g smooth peanut butter

½ teaspoon ground cinnamon

½ teaspoon vanilla bean paste or powder

3 tablespoons maple syrup, coconut nectar or monk fruit syrup

CRUST

3 tablespoons melted coconut oil, plus extra for greasing

3 tablespoons maple syrup, coconut nectar or monk fruit syrup

60 g (½ cup) cacao powder

120 g (2 cups) shredded coconut

TO SERVE

1 tablespoon cacao powder, sifted

3 tablespoons chopped roasted peanuts

75 g Luke's Chocolate (see page 150), peeled into small curls using a vegetable peeler (optional)

125 ml (½ cup) Whipped Coconut Cream (see page 153) (optional)

Preheat the oven to 180°C. Line the base of an 18 cm loose-bottomed fluted tart tin with baking paper and grease with coconut oil.

To make the crust, mix the melted coconut oil and your sweetener of choice in a bowl. Whisk in the cacao powder to incorporate, then stir in the shredded coconut. Spoon the mixture into the prepared tin and use your fingers to press it into the base and side in an even layer. Bake for 15–18 minutes, or until firm, crunchy and crispy around the edge, then remove from the oven and set aside to cool.

Warm the coconut cream in a small saucepan over medium heat. Once hot, remove the pan from the heat, add the chocolate and stir until the chocolate has melted down completely and is incorporated. Add the peanut butter, cinnamon, vanilla and your sweetener of choice and whisk well, then pour the mixture over the cooled base and refrigerate for 1 hour to set.

When ready to serve, dust with the cacao powder and scatter over the peanuts and chocolate curls (if using). Cut into slices with a warm knife and serve with some whipped coconut cream, if desired.

'KITKAT CHUNKY' BARS

Most of us are familiar with the thin set of chocolate-coated wafers that make up a traditional KitKat, right? But this little delight is modelled on its 'Chunky' form – a more recent invention that sees one large, thick finger of crunchy wafer doused in a generous quantity of that same delicious chocolate. My take on things coats a crunchy, light golden coconut cookie in a thick dark chocolate, and it's the closest I think a healthy version can get to the original. Don't believe me? Just try it and see for yourself.

MAKES 12 BARS

270 g (2 cups) coconut flour
375 ml (1½ cups) melted coconut oil
3 tablespoons maple syrup, coconut nectar or monk fruit syrup
1 teaspoon vanilla bean paste or powder
pinch of sea salt
300 g (2 cups) roughly chopped Luke's Chocolate (see page 150)

Preheat the oven to 180°C. Line a 20 cm square baking tin and a large plate or tray that will fit in your freezer with baking paper.

Add all the ingredients except the chocolate to a bowl and whisk together well. Spoon the mixture into the prepared tin and bake for 10–12 minutes, or until golden brown around the edges. Remove from the oven and leave to cool completely, then cut into 12 evenly sized bars. Arrange the bars on the prepared plate or tray, transfer to the freezer and leave for 30 minutes to chill and firm.

Melt the chocolate in a small saucepan over low heat, stirring as you go, until thick and creamy. Remove from the heat and leave to cool slightly so that it is still runny but not super hot.

Remove your chilled biscuit fingers from the freezer. Using your fingers, dip one of the bars briefly into the chocolate to coat completely, then place the bar back on the plate or tray. Repeat with the remaining bars, then transfer the tray to the freezer for 5 minutes for the chocolate to set. Return the chocolate to the stove and keep warm over low heat.

Once the first layer of chocolate has had a chance to set, dip the bars back in the chocolate as before, then transfer to the fridge until ready to serve.

The bars will keep in the fridge for up to 1 week or in the freezer for up to 3 months.

Chilli-spiced
MACADAMIA BITES

Macadamia nuts are such awesome little nutrient powerhouses, which is why I love using them in recipes like this. Make these up and you'll have a healthy snack packed with good fats that will keep sugar cravings at bay and have you feeling fuller for longer. That's a win-win, in my book.

MAKES 30 BITES

135 g (1 cup) macadamia nut butter, chilled

230 g (1 cup) coconut butter

125 ml (½ cup) melted coconut oil

125 ml (½ cup) maple syrup, coconut nectar or monk fruit syrup

¼ teaspoon ground cinnamon

¼ teaspoon cayenne pepper (add extra if you like things spicy!)

30 large macadamia nuts, plus extra chopped macadamia nuts

300 g (2 cups) roughly chopped Luke's Chocolate (see page 150)

Line a baking tray with baking paper.

Place the macadamia nut butter, coconut butter, coconut oil, your sweetener of choice, cinnamon and cayenne pepper in a food processor and blitz until smooth. Transfer to the fridge and leave for 15 minutes to firm up.

Spoon a teaspoon-sized amount of the chilled macadamia and coconut mixture into your hand and roll it around an individual macadamia nut. Place it on the prepared tray and repeat with the remaining macadamias and macadamia mixture, then transfer the tray to the fridge and chill for 15 minutes, or until firm.

Melt the chocolate in a small saucepan over low heat, stirring as you go, until thick and creamy. Remove from the heat and leave to cool slightly so that it is still runny but not super hot.

Using your fingers, lower one of the chilled macadamia bites into the chocolate to coat completely. Carefully remove the ball with a spoon and place it back on the tray, then repeat with the rest. Scatter over the extra chopped macadamias, then return the tray to the fridge to set. (I sometimes make up extra chocolate and do a few rounds of this to make the chocolate extra thick!)

Store the bites in a suitable airtight container in the fridge for up to 1 week or in the freezer for up to 3 months.

HEALTH TIP *Macadamia nuts contain protein and fibre, along with high amounts of beneficial fats. Together, these nutrients can help us feel fuller for longer as the fats take a while to digest, while the protein and fibre help prevent the swings in blood-sugar levels that can make us feel hungry.*

SPICED ROASTED PINEAPPLE
with MACADAMIA CRUNCH

I love this simple dish, which celebrates one of this country's most iconic fruits – the golden pineapple – and teams it with macadamia nuts for a dessert that screams Aussie summer. The whole family will enjoy this one, trust me.

SERVES 4

80 g (½ cup) macadamia nuts, roughly chopped

125 ml (½ cup) maple syrup, coconut nectar or monk fruit syrup

2 teaspoons coconut sugar

1 cm piece of ginger, peeled and finely grated

250 g (1 cup) coconut yoghurt or Whipped Coconut Cream (see page 153)

1 pineapple, peeled, cored and cut into wedges

1 tablespoon melted coconut oil

1 small handful of mint leaves, roughly chopped

3 tablespoons coconut flakes, toasted

Line a large tray with baking paper.

Add the chopped macadamia nuts to a small frying pan over medium–high heat and toast for 2–3 minutes, or until lightly browned. Add your sweetener of choice and cook, shaking the pan constantly, for a further 1–2 minutes, or until the nuts are coated in the syrup and the mixture has thickened slightly. Pour the mixture onto the prepared tray in a thin layer and leave to cool and set, then break into small chunks. Set aside.

Combine the coconut sugar, ginger and coconut yoghurt or whipped coconut cream in a small bowl and stir well. Refrigerate until needed.

Heat a barbecue grill plate to medium–hot or place a chargrill pan over medium–high heat. Brush the pineapple wedges with the coconut oil, transfer to the barbecue or pan and cook for 3–5 minutes on all sides, or until lovely and golden.

To serve, divide the pineapple among plates, dollop over the ginger yoghurt or cream and top with the macadamia crunch, mint leaves and coconut flakes.

TIP *Did you know that whole pineapples should initially be stored at room temperature? It is only once they're cut that you need to store the pieces in the fridge in an airtight container.*

BLUEBERRY 'BOUNTY' BARS

Growing up as a kid, I absolutely loved Bounty bars, and they were one of my all-time favourite treats for the way home from school. One thing I always felt the original lacked, though, was a burst of delicious fruit flavour – something I've changed here with the addition of yummy, nutritious blueberries to really take things to the next level.

MAKES 12 BARS

90 g (1 cup) desiccated coconut

155 g (1 cup) blueberries, fresh or frozen and thawed

125 ml (½ cup) melted coconut oil

3 tablespoons coconut cream

1 teaspoon vanilla bean paste or powder

1 tablespoon maple syrup, coconut nectar or monk fruit syrup

300 g (2 cups) roughly chopped Luke's Chocolate (see page 150)

Place all the ingredients except the chocolate in a food processor and pulse until combined.

Tip the mixture into a bowl, transfer to the freezer and leave to chill for 30 minutes, or until firm enough to shape with your hands.

Once chilled, divide the mixture into 12 evenly sized pieces. Using your hands, mould each piece into a bar shape, then arrange the bars on a tray lined with baking paper. Return to the freezer for 30 minutes to set completely.

For the chocolate coating, melt the chocolate in a small saucepan over low heat, stirring, until thick and creamy. Remove from the heat and leave to cool slightly so that it is still runny but not super hot.

Using your fingers, dip one of the chilled coconut bars briefly into the chocolate to coat completely, then place the bar back on the plate or tray. Repeat with the remaining bars, then return them to the fridge until the chocolate is set and these 'bounty' bars are ready to be devoured!

The bounty bars will keep in the fridge for up to 1 week or in the freezer for up to 3 months.

TIP *You'll see in this picture I have poured a thick layer of the chocolate over the top before completing the dipping process. This results in a thicker, chunkier chocolate coating on top. To do the same, simply spoon the chocolate onto the prepared chilled blueberry and coconut bars, place in the freezer for 10 minutes to firm up, then dunk as per the instructions above. Thank me later!*

Beautiful Birthday Cake

*This easy-to-make chocolate cake is unbelievably decadent, rich and moist. I have called it
a beautiful birthday cake because, quite simply, it's so good that it definitely deserves to
be a special birthday treat. Try it for yourself and you'll soon see why.*

SERVES 12

300 g (3 cups) almond meal
125 g (1 cup) arrowroot or
 tapioca flour
3 tablespoons coconut flour
280 g (1½ cups) coconut sugar
185 g (1½ cups) cacao powder
2 teaspoons gluten-free baking
 powder
1 teaspoon sea salt
4 Flax Eggs (see page 31)
125 ml (½ cup) melted coconut
 oil, cooled, plus extra for
 greasing
375 ml (1½ cups) coconut milk
250 ml (1 cup) filtered water
1 tablespoon apple cider vinegar
1 teaspoon vanilla bean paste
 or powder

CHOCOLATE FROSTING
560 g (4 cups) granulated or
 powdered coconut sugar, plus
 extra if needed
125 g (1 cup) cacao powder
125 ml (½ cup) coconut oil
125 ml (½ cup) almond milk
 or coconut milk, plus extra
 if needed
1 teaspoon vanilla bean paste or
 powder

TO DECORATE (OPTIONAL)
fresh raspberries
freeze-dried raspberries
shards of Luke's Chocolate (see
 page 150)

Preheat the oven to 180°C. Grease the bases and sides of three
20 cm springform cake tins with coconut oil and line the bottoms
with baking paper.

Add the dry ingredients to a large bowl and mix well to combine.
In a separate bowl, whisk together the wet ingredients. Add the wet
ingredients to the dry ingredients and whisk well for 1–2 minutes to
create your lovely cake batter.

Using a spoon, evenly distribute the batter among the three prepared
tins, transfer to the oven and bake for 30–35 minutes, or until a
skewer inserted in the centre of each sponge comes out clean.
Remove from the oven and leave to cool slightly in the tins before
turning out onto wire racks to cool completely.

For the chocolate frosting, add all the ingredients to a stand mixer
and mix on low speed for 30 seconds. Once the ingredients have
started to combine, slowly increase the speed to high and blend for
a further 1 minute. Check the consistency at this point and tweak as
desired, adding a little more milk to thin it out slightly or a little more
coconut sugar if you would prefer it a little thicker.

Once the cakes have completely cooled, assemble the birthday cake
by stacking the sponges one on top of the other, adding a quarter or
so of the chocolate frosting between each layer. Slather the remaining
frosting over the top of the cake and decorate with fresh and
freeze-dried raspberries and shards of chocolate, if desired.

TIP *If you'd like to cover this entire cake with frosting, make a
double batch of the frosting and use it to coat the side also.*

Perfect
PEANUT FUDGE

Ever feel like you need something a little sweet to keep you going between meals or to have on hand when you're on the go, but can't be bothered with anything that requires loads of ingredients and fiddly prep time? Well then, this perfect peanut fudge is for you! It's rich, decadent and decidedly moreish. It also keeps for ages, so is ideal for making up in a big batch like this.

MAKES 18 PIECES

460 g (2 cups) coconut butter, melted

500 g (2 cups) smooth peanut butter

125 ml (½ cup) melted coconut oil

3 tablespoons maple syrup, coconut nectar or monk fruit syrup

pinch of sea salt, plus extra to serve

1 teaspoon vanilla bean paste or powder

2 tablespoons crushed roasted peanuts

Line a 20 cm square cake tin with baking paper.

Place the coconut butter, peanut butter, coconut oil and your sweetener of choice in a food processor and blitz until well combined. Scrape down the side with a spatula, add the salt and vanilla and blitz again briefly, then pour the mixture into the prepared tin and spread it out in an even layer. Sprinkle the crushed peanuts over the mixture, then transfer to the freezer and leave for 20 minutes, or until set firm.

Remove the fudge from the freezer and lift it from the tin by pulling on the edges of the baking paper. Using a hot knife, cut the fudge into 18 even diamonds or squares. Sprinkle over some extra sea salt, if you like, and enjoy immediately.

Leftovers can be stored in an airtight container in the fridge for up to 10 days or in the freezer for up to 1 month. (If frozen, leave at room temperature for 5–10 minutes to soften before eating for best texture and flavour.)

TIP *If you add too much sweetener the mixture can seize up and get a little thick. It's no big problem, though – just thin it out with a bit more melted coconut oil and you'll be sorted.*

PUMPKIN *and* OLIVE OIL MUFFINS

I think muffins are the most wonderful way to get extra vegetables into your day as they are fuss free and quick and easy to make. Make up a batch of these and you'll be sorted for snack options that tick both the slightly sweet and savoury boxes – the perfect balance in my opinion.

MAKES 6 LARGE OR 9 REGULAR MUFFINS

1½ Flax Eggs (see page 31)
2 tablespoons mashed very ripe banana (about ½ banana)
185 g (¾ cup) Pumpkin Puree (see page 18)
105 g (⅔ cup) coconut sugar
3 tablespoons extra-virgin olive oil, plus extra for greasing and drizzling
1 teaspoon vanilla bean paste or powder
3 tablespoons maple syrup, coconut nectar or monk fruit syrup
2 teaspoons bicarbonate of soda
¼ teaspoon sea salt
1 teaspoon ground cinnamon
½ teaspoon ground nutmeg
125 ml (½ cup) filtered water
100 g (1 cup) almond meal
125 g (1 cup) arrowroot or tapioca flour
3 tablespoons coconut flour

CRUMBLY TOP (OPTIONAL)
3 tablespoons granulated coconut sugar
2 tablespoons almond meal
2 tablespoons arrowroot or tapioca flour
2 tablespoons roughly chopped pecans
1 tablespoon extra-virgin olive oil
½ teaspoon ground cinnamon

Preheat the oven to 180°C and lightly grease a large 6-hole or standard 9-hole muffin tin with oil or line it with paper cases.

Place the flax eggs and mashed banana in a large bowl and gently whisk to combine, leaving some small chunks of banana for lovely texture. Add the pumpkin puree, coconut sugar, olive oil, vanilla and sweetener of your choice and whisk for 1 minute, then stir in the bicarb, salt, cinnamon and nutmeg. Pour in the water, whisking as you go, until well combined, then add the almond meal, arrowroot or tapioca flour and coconut flour and stir just enough to form a thick, scoop-able batter.

Divide the batter evenly among the muffin holes. If you're making the crumbly top, combine all the ingredients in a bowl and mix with your hands or a fork to a wet sand-like texture, then generously top the muffins with it.

Bake regular-sized muffins for 30 minutes or large muffins for 35–40 minutes, or until the tops are golden brown and a skewer inserted in the centre of a muffin comes out completely clean. Leave to cool in the tin for 5 minutes, then transfer to a wire rack. Enjoy warm or at room temperature with a generous drizzle of extra-virgin olive oil.

TIP *Once completely cooled, these muffins are best stored in an airtight container at room temperature for 3–4 days and can be frozen for up to 3 months.*

NO-BAKE ZESTY CHEESECAKE

*I absolutely love this cheesecake recipe. The citrus adds a really refreshing element,
plus it doesn't require any baking, so you'll have a creamy and delicious dessert
to enjoy with no fuss and in no time at all.*

SERVES 10-12

CRUST

125 ml (½ cup) maple syrup,
coconut nectar or monk fruit
syrup, plus extra if needed

125 ml (½ cup) chilled coconut
oil, plus extra if needed

45 g (½ cup) desiccated coconut,
plus extra if needed

100 g (1 cup) pecans

pinch of sea salt

FILLING

200 g (1¼ cups) cashew nuts,
soaked overnight in cold water,
drained

1 teaspoon vanilla bean paste
or powder

1 tablespoon orange or lemon
zest, plus extra if needed

juice of 1½ lemons

1 tablespoon melted coconut oil

3 tablespoons maple syrup,
coconut nectar or monk fruit
syrup, plus extra if needed

175 g (¾ cup) coconut yoghurt,
plus extra if needed

¼ teaspoon sea salt

TO SERVE

Whipped Coconut Cream (see
page 153)

lightly crushed berries

finely grated citrus zest

Line an 18 cm springform cake tin with baking paper.

To make the crust, blitz all the ingredients in a food processor to
form a rough dough. Check the dough by taking a little of it and
squeezing it between your fingers to see if it sticks together. If it's too
dry, add more coconut oil or sweetener; if it's too wet, add a little
more desiccated coconut.

Spoon the crust mixture into the prepared tin and use your
fingers to press it into the base and side in an even layer to cover
completely. Transfer to the freezer and leave for 30 minutes, or
until set.

While the crust is setting, make the filling. Place all the ingredients
in the food processor and blitz for 2 minutes, stopping and scraping
down the side occasionally as you go, until very creamy and smooth.
Taste and adjust the flavour as needed, adding more of your chosen
sweetener for sweetness, coconut yoghurt for tanginess, or lemon or
orange zest for citrus flavour.

Pour the filling into the chilled crust and gently tap the tin a few times
on the bench to release any air bubbles. Cover loosely with baking
paper and freeze for at least 6 hours, or until firm.

When ready to serve, remove the cake from the freezer and leave
for 20–30 minutes at room temperature to thaw slightly. Slice with
a warm knife and enjoy as is or topped with whipped coconut cream,
crushed berries and citrus zest.

TIP *Any leftovers will keep in an airtight container in the fridge (for
a softer cheesecake) for 4-5 days, or in the freezer for up to 1 month.*

REALLY GOOD *Rocky Road*

I love this quick and easy version of rocky road. It is especially great to make if you have a heap of my chocolate from page 150 left over, as all you need to do is pair it with your favourite nuts and seeds for the ultimate indulgence. Use this recipe as a general guide, mixing and matching it to whatever you have in your pantry.

MAKES 16 PIECES

80 g (½ cup) macadamia nuts
70 g (½ cup) pistachio kernels
50 g (½ cup) pecans
80 g (½ cup) Brazil nuts
30 g (½ cup) flaked coconut
450 g (3 cups) roughly chopped
   Luke's Chocolate (see page 150)
15 g (½ cup) freeze-dried
   blueberries
15 g (½ cup) freeze-dried
   raspberries

Line a 20 cm square cake tin with baking paper.

Place the nuts in a large frying pan over medium heat and toast, tossing to keep them moving so they don't burn, for 4–5 minutes, or until golden brown and aromatic. Remove from the pan and set aside to cool.

Place the flaked coconut in the pan and toast, tossing, for 1–2 minutes, or until golden, then remove from the pan and add to your toasted nuts. Mix well.

Melt the chocolate in a small saucepan over low heat, stirring as you go, until thick and creamy. Remove from the heat and allow to cool slightly and thicken up.

Add the nut and coconut mixture along with the freeze-dried blueberries and raspberries to the prepared tin and spread them out in an even layer. Pour over the melted chocolate and transfer to the fridge for 30 minutes to set.

To serve, cut into 16 chunky pieces with a warm sharp knife and devour. Store any leftovers wrapped in baking paper in an airtight container in the fridge for up to 1 week or in the freezer for up to 3 months.

TIP *Freeze-dried blueberries and raspberries are popping up more and more in health food stores and supermarkets. They work wonderfully here as they keep the water content of these bars to a minimum, but if you can't find them, no worries – you can totally use fresh or frozen and thawed berries instead.*

CONVERSION CHARTS

Measuring cups and spoons may vary slightly from one country to another, but the difference is generally not enough to affect a recipe. All cup and spoon measures are level.

One Australian metric measuring cup holds 250 ml (8 fl oz), one Australian tablespoon holds 20 ml (4 teaspoons) and one Australian metric teaspoon holds 5 ml. North America, New Zealand and the UK use a 15 ml (3-teaspoon) tablespoon.

LENGTH

METRIC	IMPERIAL
3 mm	⅛ inch
6 mm	¼ inch
1 cm	½ inch
2.5 cm	1 inch
5 cm	2 inches
18 cm	7 inches
20 cm	8 inches
23 cm	9 inches
25 cm	10 inches
30 cm	12 inches

LIQUID MEASURES

ONE AMERICAN PINT	ONE IMPERIAL PINT
500 ml (16 fl oz)	600 ml (20 fl oz)

CUP	METRIC	IMPERIAL
⅛ cup	30 ml	1 fl oz
¼ cup	60 ml	2 fl oz
⅓ cup	80 ml	2½ fl oz
½ cup	125 ml	4 fl oz
⅔ cup	160 ml	5 fl oz
¾ cup	180 ml	6 fl oz
1 cup	250 ml	8 fl oz
2 cups	500 ml	16 fl oz
2¼ cups	560 ml	20 fl oz
4 cups	1 litre	32 fl oz

DRY MEASURES

The most accurate way to measure dry ingredients is to weigh them. However, if using a cup, add the ingredient loosely to the cup and level with a knife; don't compact the ingredient unless the recipe requests 'firmly packed'.

METRIC	IMPERIAL
15 g	½ oz
30 g	1 oz
60 g	2 oz
125 g	4 oz (¼ lb)
185 g	6 oz
250 g	8 oz (½ lb)
375 g	12 oz (¾ lb)
500 g	16 oz (1 lb)
1 kg	32 oz (2 lb)

OVEN TEMPERATURES

CELSIUS	FAHRENHEIT	CELSIUS	GAS MARK
100°C	200°F	110°C	¼
120°C	250°F	130°C	½
150°C	300°F	140°C	1
160°C	325°F	150°C	2
180°C	350°F	170°C	3
200°C	400°F	180°C	4
220°C	425°F	190°C	5
		200°C	6
		220°C	7
		230°C	8
		240°C	9
		250°C	10

THANKS

Well, Mary, when I see your name pop up on my phone on a casual Friday afternoon I know you've got something exciting to say. And this time it wasn't just the usual epic banter about our favourite TV shows, but the incredible beginning of this wonderful book. I remember finishing the call with you that sunny afternoon and walking down to the beach and letting out a little squeal of excitement about what was to come, and this book has certainly exceeded my expectations. Thanks for believing in this journey and coming along for the ride with me.

Jane, what a joy it has been to join forces with you again after having had such a wonderful time working on *Eat Clean* together, when I first joined the divine Plum family. As my book babies have grown and developed throughout the past few years, it has been a joy to see you and your family thrive and grow also. I absolutely love how this book is something you can wholly incorporate into your life, with some of your favourite ingredients celebrated in the way that you love to eat.

Ash, you're an absolute star! When I met you working on *Smart Carbs*, I was secretly crossing my fingers we would get to do another project together and, huzzah, you were along for the ride on this one. I'm so glad you helped bring this book together and that we got to hang out and share in all the yumminess on set.

Although the above three superstars get a special mention, this book wouldn't have been possible without the entire Plum/Pan Macmillan family. There is an enormous team of hard-working humans who take this book from just another cookbook to an incredible cookbook, far and wide around the world. In particular, the sensational and talented Charlotte Ree and the entire publicity team work tirelessly in securing vital exposure, while the sales reps and crew at HQ make sure this book is as easily accessible as possible, allowing my healthy recipes to reach more happy tastebuds.

Thank you to Caroline and Rachael, who took my manuscript and cooked each dish with love, care and incredible talent, taking each and every recipe to the next level for the beautiful images you see throughout this book. The energy you brought to the shoot was really special, supportive and inspiring, both professionally and personally. Please know your hard work never went unnoticed and I am super grateful for everything you've done to bring this book together.

A massive shout out and thank you to Deb Kaloper. What a joy it was to finally get to work with you properly after all these years. Having followed you on social media for so long and having been such a fan of what you do, it was a delight to have you style this book. You hit the brief spot on and brought your very cool Cali' vibe each and every day. Hanging out with you on set felt like I was sitting on Ocean Avenue, Santa Monica, just hanging with a mate watching the waves come in – such a good energy.

Marky Mark, this makes book number four together, brother, and I wouldn't have it any other way. You get the job done in the most seamless and easy manner, and every photo you take feels like 'the one'! It's always so hard to choose a favourite. A particular mention has to go to your performance on *The House of Wellness* special with some of the best acting I have seen since Daryl Somers at the Logies in the 1980s.

One of the most exciting parts about making a book is bringing together the photos, words graphics, fonts and the all-important cover. Well, Kirby, your talent continues to shine through with each book we do together. Thanks for making this POP in all the best ways.

To Simon, who does a brilliant job of editing my words. You've got the most incredible eye for detail and it's always a joy to work with such a succinct, efficient and positive guy. Congratulations on the growing family, I look forward to continuing to work with you, buddy.

To the bookstores, booksellers and online retailers who get my books into your hands. Your support and personal words of recommendation, while placing my books in prime positions in stores (cover facing, wink-wink!), allow my books to shine. Thanks for continuing to support this adventure; it wouldn't be possible without you.

As for my family, friends and nearest and dearest loved ones, you know who you are, and it is your belief in me that makes this possible. Thanks for always having my back. I love you.

And finally, to my readers and followers, new and old. What a road it has been together, from Kitchen HQ on *My Kitchen Rules* to this, my tenth book. By supporting me, being open to my message of health and happiness and cooking my recipes, you've allowed me to spread my passion far and wide. I am forever grateful. I'd be honoured if you stayed on this journey with me for this book and beyond. I hope I have made an impact on your life and if you allow me to, I would like to continue to support your health journey.

 xx

INDEX

A PLUM BOOK

First published in 2019 by Pan Macmillan Australia Pty Ltd
This edition published in 2020 by Pan Macmillan Australia Pty Ltd
Level 25, 1 Market Street,
Sydney, NSW 2000, Australia

Level 3, 112 Wellington Parade,
East Melbourne, Victoria 3002, Australia

Design and typesetting by Kirby Armstrong
Editing by Simon Davis
Index by Helena Holmgren
Photography by Mark Roper
Prop and food styling by Deb Kaloper
Food preparation by Caroline Griffiths and Rachael Lane
Colour reproduction by Splitting Image Colour Studio
Printed and bound in China by Imago Printing International Limited

A CIP catalogue record for this book is available from the National Library of Australia.

10 9 8 7 6 5 4 3 2 1